Baltimore Painted Furniture 1800-1840

Introduction and Commentary   by William Voss Elder, III

The Baltimore Museum of Art

Baltimore Painted Furniture 1800-1840
Dates of the exhibition:
The Baltimore Museum of Art
18 April - 4 June 1972

Cover design: detail from cat. no. 52
Flyleaf: detail from cat. no. 41
Title page: detail from cat. no. 3

The publication of this book is made
possible through the assistance
of Alex. Brown & Sons.

Copyright © 1972
The Baltimore Museum of Art
Art Museum Drive, Baltimore, Maryland 21218
Printed in the United States of America

Library of Congress Catalogue Card No.
72-77869
SBN 0-912298-25-1

LIST OF LENDERS

Mr. and Mrs. J. Hollis Albert, Jr.
Mr. and Mrs. Hugh Benet, Jr.
Colonial Dames of America, Chapter I
Mr. and Mrs. Thomas T. Fell
James M. Goode
Mr. and Mrs. Benjamin H. Griswold, III
Hampton National Site, National Park Service,
    United States Department of the Interior
Mr. and Mrs. William M. Hanna
Peter Hill
The Reverend and Mrs. S. Janney Hutton
Mr. and Mrs. Richard A. Jamison
Mr. and Mrs. Henry W. Keating
The Maryland Historical Society
Mr. and Mrs. William M. Maynadier
The Metropolitan Museum of Art
Moses Myers House of the Chrysler Museum, Norfolk
Mr. and Mrs. John M. Myers
Mr. and Mrs. Edgar Nash, III
William Hughlett Naylor
National Society of the Colonial Dames of America
    in the State of Maryland
Martha Sprigg Poole
Katherine Riggs Poole
Mrs. William D. Poultney
Mr. and Mrs. James I. Randall

A museum takes its signals from the achievements of the few, and the celebration of those accomplishments is through sharing them with others. This catalogue and the exhibition of *Baltimore Painted Furniture 1800-1840* thus become proud moments for our community and our Museum. They present an overview of the workmanship of local cabinetmakers and decorative artists during the period of Baltimore's greatest growth as a commercial and cultural center. A number of the objects are part of the Museum's collections, while others remain in the families of the original owners. In an age of so much forceful breaking from tradition, it is reassuring to have personal and institutional pride which values the past, studies it and learns from it. A related sense of history was in itself a factor in the development of the decorative motifs of this furniture, with its self-conscious references to classical antiquity.

Our ability to achieve a project of this scope is largely due to the amiable goodwill of the various lenders (listed elsewhere), who have parted with their furniture so that it could be studied and displayed. We are especially grateful to Alex. Brown & Sons for their generous support which makes possible the scope of this catalogue. Greatest thanks are due to William Voss Elder, III, Chairman of the Museum's Curatorial Division and Curator of Decorative Arts, who has organized the exhibition, assembled the catalogue and written the introduction and commentary. His scholarly insights and abilities enable the Museum to celebrate the accomplishments of Baltimore's past as a signal of hope that the work of the present will be the source of pride for the future.

Tom L. Freudenheim
Director

ACKNOWLEDGMENTS

Approximately one-third of the pieces in this exhibition are from the Museum's collection, and most of the remaining ones are of Baltimore or Maryland ownership. In numerous instances, to complete assemblages of large sets, pieces have been acquired for loan from many different descendants of the original owner. The Museum is extremely grateful for the generosity of these private owners and the institutions that have helped to make this exhibition of Baltimore painted furniture possible.

The gathering of material for this exhibition as well as the preparation of the catalogue has in large part been possible through the tireless efforts of the Assistant Curator of Decorative Arts, M. B. Munford. An exhibition of this kind is always a joint Museum effort, but special thanks and credit must be given to Ann Boyce Harper, Managing Editor of Museum Publications, without whose direction, and most of all her patience, the production of this catalogue would have been impossible. Victor Covey, Senior Conservator, and Kay Silberfeld, Conservator, were most sympathetic to the inherent problems of painted furniture and developed feasible methods of restoration. The laborious task of searching the Baltimore City Directories from 1800-40 was done through the assistance of Anne P. Fishman who was entirely responsible for the compilation of the list of cabinetmakers and allied tradesmen at the end of this catalogue.

For their time, patience, and skill we are also deeply indebted to Stephens Berge and John H. Hill who under the direction of the Museum's Conservation Department treated and restored many of the pieces of furniture included here. We also greatly benefit from the counsel of Harry D. Berry, Jr., who undertook and in many instances expedited the necessary cabinetmaking repairs and restorations.

The excellent photographs produced herein are the work of the Museum Photographer, Duane Suter. The necessary aid and involvement of the Museum's Installation Department was ably assumed by Margaret M. Powell, Installionist, and Robert A. Zimmerman, Designer. Frances M. Bunn and Audrey M. Frantz are to be thanked for typing all of the material for this catalogue.

We are also especially grateful for the library and research services provided by the George Peabody Branch and the Maryland Room of the Enoch Pratt Free Library, The Maryland Historical Society, The Johns Hopkins University, the Walters Art Gallery, and The Henry Francis du Pont Winterthur Museum.

W. V. E. III

Baltimore painted furniture of the period 1800-40 is a unique contribution to American cabinetmaking and was unparalleled in its own time by products of other major east coast cabinetmaking centers. Although in mahogany and other hardwood furniture Baltimore chairmakers and cabinetmakers followed the same sequence of style and decoration in the early 19th century as Philadelphia and New York, they continued to produce painted furniture on a scale not attained or perhaps not desired in other American cabinetmaking centers where painted furniture simply does not exist in the quantity or quality of Baltimore.

The earliest examples of Baltimore painted furniture are in the classical style of Hepplewhite and Sheraton. In England, in the latter half of the 18th century, painted furniture enjoyed a great vogue and was as fully acceptable as mahogany furniture in the best rooms of English houses. This vogue was transported to America, and painted or fancy chairs are mentioned in inventories of American houses in the late 18th and early 19th century — a most notable example being a reference to "black and gold" chairs in Thomas Jefferson's own handwritten inventory of the White House in 1809. These chairs could well have been American, made in the Sheraton fancy chair tradition.

Baltimore in the early 19th century was America's fastest growing city and, for a brief period of time, the nation's third most populous urban center after Philadelphia and New York. Elaborately ornamented furniture could well have pleased the taste of Baltimore's new prosperous merchant class. By the 1820's and 1830's when the architectural countenance of the City was being changed by such great classical revival architects as Benjamin H. Latrobe, Maximilien Godefroy and Robert Mills, Baltimore furniture was made and decorated in a classical, archaeological style that reflected this new taste.

Whereas, in the first two decades of the 19th century it was considered fashionable to paint and decorate surfaces, the intent in the 1820's and 1830's was somewhat different. In many instances the wood, instead of being completely painted with a single ground color, was grained to simulate rosewood, indicating a desire to imitate an expensive and at that time fashionable wood. It is of interest to note that examples of Baltimore furniture in the true classical, archaeological style occur often, if not exclusively, in painted furniture. The methods of applying decoration also changed. In the early 19th century, the polychrome and gilt decoration was usually freehand and was applied over a colored ground. Varnish was used as the vehicle for both the polychrome pigments and the gilt decoration, a technique described by Thomas Sheraton in the sections entitled "Of Painting Chairs" and "Of Drawing Lines on Chairs" *(The Cabinet Dictionary,* 1803 edition, pp. 424-26). He makes reference to the composition and preparation of paints for the ground colors and striping of chairs. The colors were to be "partly diluted with good turpentine varnish and partly copal."

In the later examples of the classical, archaeological style there was frequently an even mixture of stenciling and freehand brushwork in the gilt and polychrome decoration, or, in some instances, especially prevalent in the fruit and foliage motifs, a complete stenciled technique was used and the design was enriched by freehand bronzing.

Other Baltimore furniture being produced during the period 1800-40 is not closely related in the use of decorative motifs to Baltimore painted furniture. The characteristics of the well-known and richly inlaid Baltimore mahogany furniture in the classical style of Hepplewhite and Sheraton have been isolated and defined in the Baltimore Museum's 1947 exhibition, "Baltimore Furniture: the Work of Baltimore and Annapolis Cabinetmakers from 1760-1810." Later in the 19th century there was an identifiable local cabinetmaking style, the equivalent of the well-known style of Duncan Phyfe. Chairs, pedestal-based card and dining room tables, sideboards, etc. in the best mahogany were produced in great volume in Baltimore from 1810 to 1840. In the 1840's and later, furniture in the heavier "pillar and scroll" style was made after designs of John Hall, Baltimore's counterpart of Meeks and Sons of New York, and others.

The best known and most important set of early 19th-century Baltimore painted furniture, originally owned by the Baltimore merchant, John B. Morris, is attributed to the brothers Hugh and John Finlay by the existence of a family memorandum (see cat. nos. 3-5) and is believed to have been made about 1805. Thirteen pieces comprise the set, and its unique decoration may well mark the beginning of a preference for painted furniture in 19th-century Baltimore. Hugh and John Finlay were born in Ireland and received their cabinetmaking training there. They arrived in Baltimore presumably in the last decade of the 18th century and were engaged in the cabinetmaking and fancy chair business for many years. The number of listings in the Baltimore City Directories for the Finlays (both together and apart) and the various locations of their shop on North Gay Street in the center of Baltimore's cabinet-making industry (see p. 106) indicate that they were prosperous in the cabinetmaking business and would have ascended to the respectable citizenship typical of the leading

18th- and early 19th-century craftsmen in Baltimore. The range of the Finlays' production and their specialization in painted and gilded surfaces is immediately apparent in their advertisement in the Baltimore newspaper, the *Federal Gazette & Baltimore Daily Advertiser*, on 8 November 1805:

CANE SEAT CHAIRS, SOFAS, RECESS, and WINDOW SEATS of every description and all colors, gilt, ornamented and varnished in a stile not equalled on the continent — with real Views, Fancy Landscapes, Flowers, Trophies of Music, War, Husbandry, Love, &c. &c. Also, A number of sets of new pattern Rush and Windsor Chairs and Settees; Card, Tea, Peir, Writing and Dressing Tables, with Mahogany, Satin-Wood, Painted, Japanned and real Marble Top Sideboards; Ladies' Work Wash-Stand and Candle Stands; Horse Pole, Candle and Fire Screens; Bedsteads, Bed and Window Cornices, the centers enriched with Gold and Painted Fruit, Scroll and Flower Borders of entire new patterns, the mouldings in Japan, Oil and Burnish Gold, with Beads, Twists, Nelson Balls, &c. Likewise Brackets, Girondoles and Trypods; Ladies' Needle Work, Pictures and Looking Glass Frames; old Frames Regilt; real Views taken on the spot to any dimension, in oil or watercolors; Coach, Flag and Masonic Painting; and particular attention paid to Gold Sign Lettering on Glass, Pannel or Metal. JOHN & HUGH FINLAY

N. B. Orders for the West Indies, or any port of the continent, executed with dispatch.

The Finlays may well have been the chief producers of fine Baltimore painted furniture and were most likely imitated by their contemporary Baltimore cabinetmakers. By analyzing the decoration on the Morris set and through stylistic comparisons, many other pieces of Baltimore painted furniture of the early 19th century have been attributed here to the Finlays and the characteristics of their style may serve as an index to the optimum in Baltimore painted furniture.

One of their most distinctive features is the use of architectural views as an element of decoration. The Morris set alone has seventeen views of Baltimore houses and public buildings — one on each chair, three on each settee and one on the pier table — although there is no known association between these buildings and the Morris family.

One of the Finlays' first newspaper advertisements in the *Federal Gazette and Baltimore Daily Advertiser* of 31 January 1803 makes direct reference to tables and cane seat chairs "painted and gilt in the most fanciful manner, with and without views adjacent to this city."

In an advertisement of 10 October 1804 in Baltimore's *American and Commercial Daily Advertiser,* the Finlays advise the citizens of Baltimore that they could "supply them with views on their Chairs and Furniture which they

12

alone could do, as they hold an exclusive right for that species of ornament." To date no records or legal documents have been found to support this claim. However, if proved correct, then all Baltimore furniture with architectural views would have to be attributed to the Finlays. There are two painted Baltimore tables (cat. nos. 14 & 15) and two matching side chairs (cat. no. 18) of different provenances but with architectural views and identical elements of gilt decoration. Two of these architectural views (cat. nos. 14 & 18) are duplicated on the Morris set of furniture, and all are of the same quality of painting. The gilt decoration, however, is not up to the Finlays' usual shop standards. This might indicate that the gilt decoration was not always done by the same ornamenter — a supposition supported by conservation reports (see pp. 90-91). Whether less elaborate decoration was a reflection of price or whether the various gilt ornamenters varied in experience or capabilities is not known.

The question of who was actually responsible for both the extremely delicate decoration in gilt and paint glazes on furniture from the Finlay shop as well as the panels of floral, armorial, or agricultural trophies, and the architectural views of the Baltimore houses and public buildings remains unanswered. In contemporary accounts, Hugh is mentioned as a gifted painter, and he may well be responsible for much of the decoration on the painted furniture of their shop. In one of the few documented references to Baltimore painted furniture, there appears another possibility; the name of a "Mr. Debreet" is mentioned in a letter, surviving in the Massachusetts Historical Society, written from New York on 7 December 1825 by Rembrandt Peale to Thomas Jefferson. The original letter from Jefferson to which Peale's letter is a response has not been located. Apparently Peale had received a letter from Jefferson asking his opinion on the merits of a "Mr. Debreet" at a time when Jefferson was looking for a professor of painting at the University of Virginia. Rembrandt Peale writes: "For a while he was engaged in Baltimore ornamenting Windsor chairs for Messrs. Finlay when I became acquainted with him and it is only of late that he has attempted to make pictures or landscapes. I cannot but think his practice on the chairs has been injurious to his taste." Further on in the letter Rembrandt Peale discussed the merits of the American artist Doughty and notes that he draws better than Debreet. This name certainly refers to Cornelius de Beet who is listed in the Baltimore City Directory as a fancy painter or ornamental painter for the period 1810-40 (see listing p. 103). There is a ten year period between 1819 and 1829 when de Beet is not listed in the Directories as an individual

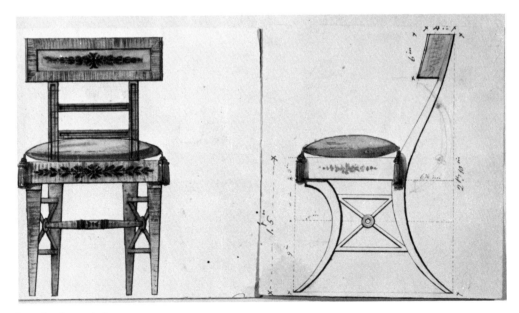

Drawing for a Chair
From the papers of Benjamin Henry Latrobe on deposit at the
Maryland Historical Society

man of business. Since Peale's letter of 1825 said that only of late had de Beet "attempted to make pictures of landscapes" — a reference to oil paintings rather than the decoration of furniture — it seems that sometime in this ten year period, perhaps from 1820 to about 1825, Cornelius de Beet was under the direct employ of the brothers Finlay. There is also another reference (Semmes, p. 111) to Mr. de Beet as "a very clever artist in oil, whose specialty, by the way, was flowers," a decorative motif that occurs frequently in Baltimore painted furniture.

In the administration of James H. Madison, Benjamin H. Latrobe remodeled the interior of the White House, and, in 1809, he turned from the struggling new city of Washington to Baltimore and to the shop of the Finlays for furniture to decorate the Oval Room of the White House. Latrobe's drawing for this furniture, with notes regarding their construction and finishing to Mr. Finlay, still exist in the collections of the Maryland Historical Society (see illus.). The design was based on the classical, archaeological style of the English designer, Thomas Hope, and others. This furniture, if produced by the Finlays, was then of a style unlike their usual line of painted furniture and one that would not be fully realized and accepted in Baltimore for perhaps another ten years. However, these furniture designs are an introduction and a bridge to the classical, archaeological style that is represented by many examples of later Baltimore painted furniture.

The origin of this new style in cabinetmaking in both England and America has been well discussed in the landmark exhibition "Classical America 1815-45" held at the Newark Museum in 1963. New discoveries in classical antiquity, renewed interest in ancient civilizations, the adoption of Greek and Roman ideologies and political thought in the formative years of our new republic, all fostered a return in style to true classical sources rather than a continuation of 18th-century classicism that had grown out of the Renaissance and the Baroque. In addition to Thomas Hope's book, *Household Furniture and Interior Decoration . . .,* published in London in 1807, the other most important design sources for the American cabinetmaker were Charles Percier and Pierre F. L. Fontaine's *Recueil de Décorations Intérieures . . .,* published in Paris in 1812, and also George Smith's *A Collection of Designs for Household Furniture . . .* of 1808, published in London.

In studying Baltimore furniture of this period it is far easier to isolate the source for furniture forms than it is for various elements of decoration. The various gilt motifs of classical anthemia, acanthus leaves, bound fasces, rosettes, sprays of leaves and acorn clusters, and winged thunderbolts

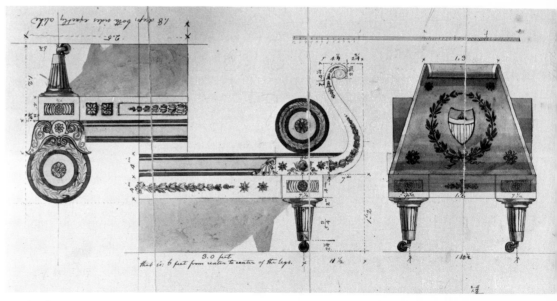

Drawing for a Settee
From the papers of Benjamin Henry Latrobe on deposit at the Maryland Historical Society

were the Baltimore cabinetmaker's substitute for ormolu mountings and, in many instances, were imitative of these designs. These repeated designs emerge as elements of a local style possibly through the influence of one large shop or painted furniture manufactory or through a shared ornamenter of furniture.

Besides the Morris set of furniture attributed to a "Mr. Findley" by a late 19th-century family memorandum and a settee (cat. no. 20) signed by Thomas Renshaw and John Barnhart, there are no other known, firmly documented pieces.

The length of the listings of cabinetmakers and allied tradesmen in the Baltimore City Directories in the period 1800-40 included here attests to the size and scale of the cabinetmaking industry in Baltimore, unfortunately not matched by any documentation of their production and individual activities. From the addresses of their shops, we can in some measure determine the quality of their works and their clientele. Of particular interest is the cabinet-maker Robert Fisher. There are numerous pieces of furniture included here which have been in the past attributed without documentation to him, and this has been discussed in the entries (cat. no. 6). The City Directory of 1800-01 reveals that he had a basement shop at 35 South Gay Street. In the City Directory of 1807, 1808 and 1810 his name continues to be listed with his shop being at 37 South Gay Street, a prestigious address. Located at the same place were Lachlan Phyfe (1807 & 1808) the brother of Duncan Phyfe and later considered to be his best carver; subsequently Thomas Renshaw (1814-15); and later the firm of Jesse L. and Jacob Hiss (1817-23). Water Street and North and South Gay Street contained the shops of Baltimore's most prosperous and fashionable cabinet and chairmakers. During the years 1810 to 1817 Robert Fisher is no longer listed as a cabinetmaker in the City Directories. However, a Robert Fisher, lumber merchant, is listed in 1817 and 1819 at the end of Spears Wharf, with a dwelling in the very respectable residential area on Pleasant Street near St. Paul's Lane. The ascendancy from cabinetmaker to lumber merchant was typical in Baltimore and other east coast 19th-century cabinetmaking centers.

Jesse Hiss, listed in the City Directory of 1816 at 37 South Gay Street, as chairmaker, went the next year in partnership with his brother Jacob until 1823. Jacob continues to be listed as a fancy chairmaker up to 1840 — one of the most extensive listings which has a direct relationship to painted furniture. Jesse Hiss was still working as a chair-maker in 1840 with a shop in Old Town, and in the 1840's the City Directories list a cabinet ware room owned by a

Philip Hiss and Austin. This Baltimore cabinetmaking firm existed into the 20th century, but unfortunately no early records survive. From the myriad list of Baltimore cabinet-makers, ornamental painters, fancy painters, chair ornamenters, etc., it would be particularly interesting to select for further research Robert Fisher and the brothers Hiss.

Even though we have been unable to add to our list of documented Baltimore painted furniture, this assemblage of eighty odd examples has isolated and defined local characteristics. From what we know, the brothers Finlay and their followers seem to dominate the style of the early 19th century. The presence of architectural views, armorial, agricultural or floral painted panels; gilt sawtooth-edged, flanking panels; gilt striped legs with cuffed bottoms; and intricately-shaped table tops and aprons, all emerge as elements of design and are typical of the examples included here. These characteristics are substantiated further in that the pieces have firm Maryland provenances or more specifically Baltimore. The furniture, considered indi-vidually, besides being the highest achievement in American painted furniture of the early 19th century, also perpetuates the excellent and elegant design typical of all Baltimore classical furniture of the same period.

In about 1820-40, a new form in painted furniture emerges. This classical, archaeological style in which the furniture forms are based on antique classical models is further recognized by a combination of stenciled and freehand gilt and polychrome decoration, most often applied on a simulated rosewood graining. Certain design motifs occur repeatedly — winged thunderbolts, anthemia, Grecian scrolls, acanthus leaves. This later Baltimore painted furniture may well represent the largest and most related group of 19th-century American furniture based on ancient Greek and Roman designs.

Although two distinct styles are illustrated in the forty year period, 1800-40, it must be remembered that, in many instances, the same cabinetmaker made furniture in both styles for a continuous clientele. One is tempted to speculate upon the domination of the Finlays and to conclude that, due to the quality of their product, a sophisticated taste in the Baltimore area was created and would, to some extent, explain the local popularity of the fashion of painted furniture.

15

Finding pieces of furniture for this exhibition has been difficult on many counts. First of all, painted furniture is an extremely fragile medium, and too many pieces of furniture that were considered and examined were found to have been ruined by needless overpainting. In addition, fully one-half of the objects included here have been subject to partial or complete restoration.

Since much painted furniture was made in sets, the pieces have been arranged chronologically rather than separated into categories. Unless there is a specific reason for an exact date, the individual pieces of furniture are listed as being made during a general time period, usually a decade.

The measurements for each piece of furniture were taken in the Museum. For chairs, the height is from the floor to the top center of the chair back; the width is of the front seat rail; and the depth is from the center of the front seat rail to the center of the rear seat rail. For corner, serving, pier or card tables (always measured with the leaf down or closed), the height is to the top-most surface — even if the top might not be of wood; the width is the greatest horizontal measurement whether it be at the front or back; and the depth is measured in the center from front to back. For benches, settees, window seats and sofas, the height would be the measurement at the highest point — either of the seat, arm or back. The depth is the measurement from front to back in the center of the front seat rail. The length is at the point of greatest length on the front or rear seat rail. If the measurements are used for comparative purposes, it should be remembered that often apparently identical chairs or tables in sets of Baltimore painted furniture may differ slightly in their dimensions.

A wood analysis has not been included, primarily because it is not necessary, as in the case of furniture of an earlier period, to prove American rather than European origin. Secondly, an examination and recognition of many of the woods used in construction of this furniture indicates in many instances that, since the finished product was to be painted rather than finished, any wood at hand would suffice for the cabinetmaker's need. Local tulip poplar was found to be used most often. Hard yellow pine, maple and oak were also found. An exception to this might be in the use of hardwoods chosen for their strength in such areas as structural supports or for the hinging of card tables.

For practical reasons, references in the catalogue entries have been shortened to include only the author's last name and page number. The more complete reference is given in the Selected Bibliography at the end of the book where the works cited are listed separately and alphabetically. Exhibition catalogues are listed alphabetically by city.

CATALOGUE AND COMMENTARY

1   **CORNER TABLE** (One of a pair) ca. 1800
Possible attribution to Hugh and John Finlay

Mahogany with satinwood inlay; painted gilt and
verre églomisé decoration; marble top

Height: 37 in.; width: 21½ in.; depth: 21½ in.

Provenance: Cohen family of Baltimore; given to
the Society by a descendant .

Lent by The Maryland Historical Society
Gift of Miss Eleanor Cohen

This corner table and the following one have
been included because of their relationship to
Baltimore painted furniture of the early 19th
century and their possible attribution to Hugh
and John Finlay. Each corner table has a central
decoration on the skirt, a *verre églomisé* panel,
here armorial trophies in gilt on a blue background. Although the derivation of such designs
as armorial trophies, musical instruments, or even
agricultural implements, can be traced to the
Sheraton tradition, the subject matter and
execution of this painted panel is related to and
repeated in polychrome decoration on Baltimore
painted furniture made by the Finlays and other
Baltimore cabinetmakers. In addition, the gilt-
banded, acanthus leaf decoration on the stile of
each of the front legs occurs in the same location
in two pieces of Baltimore painted furniture
attributed here to Hugh and John Finlay (cats.
nos. 12 and 16) . On three sides of the square
block, near the bottom of the legs of this table
at the juncture of the stretchers and above the
turned feet, a gilt rosette decoration occurs that
is also present on a pier table of the same period
(cat. no. 12) .

2 CORNER TABLE ca. 1800

Possible attribution to Hugh and John Finlay

Mahogany with satinwood inlay; painted gilt and
verre églomisé decoration; marble top

Height: 36¾ in.; width: 27⅝ in.; depth: 20¼ in.

Provenance: Hollyday family of *Readbourne,* near
Centreville, Maryland; by descent to present owner

Private Collection

With the exception of the subject matter for the
verre églomisé panel, the shaping of the stretcher
base, and the size of the urn finial, this marble-
topped corner table is of the same design as the
one preceding it (cat. no. 1) . Here the subject
matter of the panel is a winged dragon rather
than armorial trophies.

It has been suggested that perhaps these corner
tables, with blue marble tops and painted *verre
églomisé* decoration, might be from the shop of
Joseph Barry of Philadelphia. For the year 1803,
Joseph Barry is listed in the Baltimore City
Directory and his advertisement in a Baltimore
newspaper (*The Federal Gazette* and *Baltimore
Daily Advertiser*, 9 February 1803) , refers to
corner tables with marble tops. However, since
the two corner tables included here as well as
one owned by The Baltimore Museum of Art
and two such tables and a pair of pier tables
owned by Winterthur Museum (see Montgomery,
pp. 368-70; repro., pp. 368 & 69) all have Maryland
provenances and considering the short period of
time that Barry was in Baltimore, it would seem
unlikely that he was responsible for this large,
related group of furniture.

The late Dr. James Bordley in an unpublished
manuscript (Maryland Historical Society) states
that in 1803 or 1804 Hugh and John Finlay
made "in sets of four, two marble-topped corner
tables, a marble-topped pier table, and a pier
glass after a French design." The source or
documentation for Dr. Bordley's statement is
unknown. However, similarity of design and
decoration on these corner tables to other pieces
of painted furniture firmly attributed to the
Finlays would tempt to support Dr. Bordley's
claim.

3 ARMCHAIR (One of ten) ca. 1800-10
Attributed to Hugh and John Finlay

Wood painted black with gilt and polychrome
decoration

Height: 33¼ in.; width: 21¼ in.; depth: 19 in.

Provenance: Originally owned by John B. Morris of
Clermont, near Baltimore; acquired by the Museum
from descendants

Part of a set of thirteen pieces (see cat. nos. 4 & 5)

The Baltimore Museum of Art
Gift of Lydia Howard de Roth and
Nancy H. De Ford Venable
and Museum Purchase   66.26.1-10

4 SETTEE (One of a pair) ca. 1800-10
Attributed to Hugh and John Finlay

Wood painted black with gilt and polychrome
decoration

Height: 33⅝ in.; length: 50¾ in.; depth: 19⅜ in.

Provenance: Originally owned by John B. Morris of
Clermont, near Baltimore; acquired by the Museum
from descendants

Part of a set of thirteen pieces (see cat. nos. 3 & 5)

The Baltimore Museum of Art
Gift of Lydia Howard de Roth and
Nancy H. De Ford Venable
and Museum Purchase   66.26.11 & 12

5   PIER TABLE ca. 1800-10
Attributed to Hugh and John Finlay

Wood painted black with gilt and polychrome decoration

Height: 37 in.; width: 48⅜ in.; depth: 24⅛ in.

Provenance: Originally owned by John B. Morris of *Clermont*, near Baltimore; acquired by the Museum from descendants

Part of a set of thirteen pieces (see cat. nos. 3 & 4)

The Baltimore Museum of Art
Gift of Lydia Howard de Roth and
Nancy H. De Ford Venable
and Museum Purchase   66.26.13

The name Finlay has always been associated with this most important and best preserved set of Baltimore painted furniture which was believed to have been made about 1805 for John Morris, a Baltimore merchant and patriot. In the catalogue for an exhibition of Baltimore and Maryland furniture (Baltimore Museum, 1947, pp. 154-56) mention is made of a family memorandum attributing this set to a Baltimore cabinetmaker named Finlay. This memorandum now owned by the Baltimore Museum can be dated from the late 19th or early 20th century.

The thirteen-piece set consists of ten armchairs, two settees and one marble-topped pier table. Each armchair contains on its crest rail a polychrome painting of a view of a Baltimore house or public building. Three such views are found on the back of each of the settees and one on the pier table. Included in the old family memorandum attributing this set of furniture to the brothers Finlay, there is a numbered list identifying these houses and public buildings. The chairs and the settees are correspondingly marked with painted numbers on the back of the seat rail.

The architectural views on the crest rails of the chairs and settees are flanked by rectangular panels of banding in several shades of gilt glazing in a diapered design and leaf and vine motif. The vertical back supports are edged with acanthus leaf and a grapevine motif. On the center vertical, back splat, there is a polychrome painting of an armorial design of a bow and quiver. The gilt grapevine design also appears on the bottom horizontal members of the backs of

Greenwood ca. 1800-05
Philip Rogers (1749-1836) , owner
Demolished

Belvidere ca. 1790
General John Eager Howard (1752-1827) , owner
Location: near intersection of Calvert and Chase Streets
Demolished ca. 1875

the chairs and settees and on the top of the curvi-linear arm rest. The turned supports of the backs are striped in two tones of gilt as well as being ribboned in black. Gold paterae appear at the base or stiles of these turned, back supports. On the seat rail of each chair and settee, there is a polychrome oval medallion, again an armorial trophy of arrows and a quiver imposed on an oak leaf and acorn spray in gilt. The gilt paterae, ribboning and striping of the turned back supports are repeated in the front legs of the chairs and the settees. The legs terminate in spade feet in the manner of Baltimore furniture of this period. It is of interest to note that the shape of the chair back with lancet arches, illustrated in a Finlay newspaper advertisement *(Federal Gazette and Baltimore Daily Advertiser,* 24 October 1803, see p. 95) , is similar to the backs of the chairs and settees in this Morris set of Baltimore painted furniture.

The decoration on the skirt of the white marble-topped pier table repeats that of the chair and settee backs — an architectural view flanked by gilt, diapered bands enframing rectangular panels in a vine motif and, in the case of the pier table, the curved skirt is further enriched at each end by polychrome paintings of armorial, musical and agricultural trophies. Gilt paterae are repeated on the stiles of each of the legs which are accordingly striped and ribboned in the manner of other pieces of furniture in this set.

The gilt and polychrome decoration on the chairs, settees and pier table can serve as an index of design for the work of Hugh and John Finlay.

Of the seventeen houses and public buildings represented in the architectural views on this set, only two buildings survive to the present day — *Homewood* on the Johns Hopkins University campus, built 1801-02 for Charles Carroll, the son of Charles Carroll of Carrollton, and *Mount Clare,* begun about 1760 by Charles Carroll, the Barrister. Only the central portion of *Mount Clare* remains in Carroll Park here in Baltimore. All of the other buildings have been lost in the growth of the city since the early 19th century. From other surviving pictorial sources,

the rendering of these houses is unusually
accurate and, if taken as a sampling of the best
examples of Baltimore late 18th- and early 19th-
century architecture, the City and its environs
must have possessed an outstanding architectural
countenance in the early years of the 19th
century.

Bolton   ca. 1800
George Grundy (1755-1825) , owner
Location: intersection of Bolton and Hoffman Streets
Demolished in 1900

Rose Hill   1798
William Gibson (1753-1832) , owner
Location: near southeast corner of Lanvale Street and Eutaw Place
Demolished

Grace Hill
Hugh McCurdy (in Baltimore between 1790 and 1805) , owner
Demolished

Beech Hill
Robert Gilmor I (1748-1822) , owner
Location: near intersection of Saratoga and Gilmor Streets
Demolished

Willow Brook 1799
John Donnell (1754-1827) , owner
Location: corner of Mount and Hollins Streets
Demolished in 1965

St. Paul's Charity School ca. 1800
Demolished

Mt. Deposit
David Harris (ca. 1752-1809), owner
Location: near Herring Run, north of the Philadelphia Road
Demolished

Oakley
Levi Pierce (1769-1821), owner
Location: Walbrook
Demolished

Woodville
Jeremiah Yellott, owner
Demolished

Mount Clare ca. 1760
Built by Charles Carroll, the Barrister (1723-1783)
Location: Carroll Park

Banks of the City ca. 1801
Built by the Bank of Maryland, Bank of Baltimore, Office of
Discount and Deposit
Location: triangle formed by North Avenue, Bolton and
Laurens Streets
Demolished

Homewood ca. 1801-03
Charles Carroll of Homewood (1775-1825) , owner
Location: Campus of The Johns Hopkins University

The Vineyard   ca. 1799
William Gilmor (1775-1829) , owner
Location: between 28th and 29th Streets, west of
Greenmount Avenue
Demolished in 1958

Montebello   ca. 1798
General Samuel Smith (1752-1839) , owner
Location: south of 33rd Street, east of the Alameda
Demolished in 1907

Walter Dorsey House
Walter Dorsey, owner
Demolished

SIDE CHAIR (One of four) ca. 1800-10

Possible attribution to Hugh and John Finlay

Wood painted black with gilt and polychrome decoration

Height: 33½ in.; width: 19⅛ in.; depth: 15½ in.

Provenance: Buchanan family of Baltimore; purchased by the Museum from descendants

One of ten matching chairs; three at Winterthur Museum (Montgomery, pp. 451-52; repro., p. 451); two in private collections; one destroyed

Part of a set of sixteen pieces (see cat. nos. 7-9 and Montgomery, p. 453, repro., p. 452)

The Baltimore Museum of Art
George C. Jenkins Fund   69.8.2 & 3, 70.13 a & b

William Buchanan, for whom this set of painted furniture is said to have been made, moved to Baltimore from Carlisle, Pennsylvania, in 1759 and set up a shipping business. He died in 1804 and may have purchased this set of furniture shortly before his death.

These chairs and other matching pieces are, with the exception of the set made for John Morris (cat. nos. 3-5), the most elaborate and sophisticated examples of Baltimore painted furniture from the first years of the 19th century and represent one of the largest known sets. Originally numbering sixteen pieces, six are now in the collection of the Baltimore Museum (four chairs, window seat, and pier table); six are in the Winterthur Museum (three chairs, window seat, card table and settee); three are owned by the descendants of the Buchanan family (card table and two chairs). A side chair which was burned in Virginia many years ago was said to have borne the inscription of the cabinetmaker. An article entitled "Buchanan Family Reminiscences" (*Maryland Historical Society Magazine*, 1940, pp. 262-69) states that this furniture was made by Robert Crawford. Since no listing for a Baltimore cabinetmaker of that name appears in the Baltimore City Directory for the period 1800-40, this attribution would seem unlikely. Another attribution, made while part of the set was in the possession of the late Mrs. Miles White, Jr., was given to the Baltimore cabinetmaker, Robert Fisher, and has been repeated in other sources (Miller, I, p. 290; Lockwood, II, p. 311). Robert Fisher is listed in the Baltimore City Directories as a cabinetmaker and fancy chairmaker from 1800-10. Perhaps future research will substantiate this information; however, it seems more likely that the set should be associated with Hugh and John Finlay owing to the quality and similarity of design motifs to other furniture which has been firmly attributed to the Finlays. In addition, a Finlay advertisement of 1804 (*American and Commercial Daily Advertiser,* Baltimore, 10 October), states that they had the exclusive right to ornament furniture with architectural views. Although there is no known reason for their claim, such painted panels as those that appear on this set of furniture (cat. no. 8 and 9) are typical of other furniture firmly attributed to the Finlays.

Characteristic are the crest rails of the side chairs which contain central panels decorated with either musical instruments, armorial trophies or agricultural implements in polychromy (see cat. no. 10). These panels are flanked by the typical gilt, sawtooth-edged panels found on furniture attributed to the Finlays. Paterae occur on the stiles of the back supports and on the front of the seat rail, and the legs and back supports are striped with gilt — both features which are associated with the Finlay shop (see cat. no. 10).

The icicle-shaped splats are typical of Baltimore painted furniture, although not specifically Finlay, as are the spade feet on the front and rear legs. The cane seats can be removed to facilitate re-caning. Although none of these chairs retain their original caning, it is of interest to note that from the remaining paint on the underside of the seats, it can be determined that the first caning was painted a yellow, straw-like color.

7 WINDOW SEAT ca. 1800-10

Possible attribution to Hugh and John Finlay

Wood painted black with gilt and polychrome decoration

Height: 31½ in.; length: 49¼ in.; depth: 13¾ in.

Provenance: Buchanan family of Baltimore; given to the Museum by descendants

One of a matching pair; mate at Winterthur Museum (Montgomery, p. 453, repro., p. 452)

Part of a set of sixteen pieces (see cat. nos. 6, 8, 9 and Montgomery, p. 453; repro., p. 452)

The Baltimore Museum of Art
Gift of Mr. Ulric O. Hutton   72.19

The top rails of both ends of this window seat are curved to fit in and around the framing of the window recesses in one of the houses on Gay Street built by William Buchanan for his widowed daughter, Mary Allison, and her sisters, Sydney and Peggy at 17 and 19 North Gay Street (now the site of the War Memorial Plaza). From this it can be assumed that at least the window seats, if not the entire set, were made by special order.

Under the caned seat, there are three cross braces running from front to back. These curved and chamfered braces are a construction feature which will continue in Baltimore painted furniture through the 1830s and 1840s. On each of the four front legs, there is a gilt striping to resemble inlay or reeding. Paterae appear on the front rail of the seat and the stiles at each corner. Armorial and musical trophies in gilt and polychrome glazes occur in the center of each end support — a feature often associated with Hugh and John Finlay (see cat. no. 13).

The turned feet are restorations based on the matching window seat.

8   CARD TABLE ca. 1800-10

Possible attribution to Hugh and John Finlay

Wood painted black with gilt and polychrome
decoration; mahogany veneered playing surface

Height: 30⅝ in.; width: 38⅞ in.; depth: 15¼ in.

Provenance: Buchanan family of Baltimore; by
descent to the present owners

One of a matching pair; mate at Winterthur Museum
(Montgomery, p. 451; repro, p. 451)

Part of a set of sixteen pieces (see cat. nos. 6, 7, 9 and
Montgomery, p. 453; repro., p. 452)

Lent by The Reverend and Mrs. S. Janney Hutton

The painted, black background has been
enhanced by gilt decoration on the skirt in the
form of sawtooth-edged panels — a feature
associated with the shop of Hugh and John
Finlay. This motif is also repeated on the edge
of the table top. Painted gilt paterae are on the
stiles at the top of each leg. The painted, floral
panels in polychromy on the rounded corners
of the card table are similar to those on the crest
rails of the side chairs made for this same set
(cat. no. 6).

The building depicted on the central panel of
the skirt is said to be the Buchanan family's
country house, located north of Baltimore near
the Green Spring Valley. The exact location is
undetermined (*Maryland Historical Magazine*,
1940, pp. 262-69). The building on the skirt of
the matching card table at the Winterthur
Museum has not yet been identified.

9   **PIER TABLE ca. 1800-10**
Possible attribution to Hugh and John Finlay

Wood painted black with gilt and polychrome decoration

Height: 35¾ in.; width: 45¼ in.; depth: 17½ in.

Provenance: Buchanan family of Baltimore; purchased by the Museum from descendants

Part of a set of sixteen pieces (see cat. nos. 6-8 and Montgomery, p. 452; repro., p. 453)

The Baltimore Museum of Art
George C. Jenkins Fund   69.8.1

This pier table, with hollow front and rounded ends, is supported by four legs connected by arch scroll stretchers capped with an urn finial. Two tones of gilt are used for the striping on all legs, and gilt decoration is also found on the scroll stretchers and urn finial. The top surface is marbleized. The center panel on the table's skirt is a view of the two town houses built by William Buchanan for members of his family at 17 and 19 North Gay Street (see cat. no. 7); the two side painted panels have motifs of flowers and agricultural implements. Gilt, sawtooth-edged panels flank the three polychrome paintings.

The spade feet are restorations.

10 WINDOW SEAT (One of a pair) ca. 1800-10
Attributed to Hugh and John Finlay

Wood painted black with gilt and polychrome
decoration

Height: 28⅞ in.; length: 39 in.; depth: 14⅜ in.

Provenance: Macgill family of Shepherdstown,
West Virginia; by descent to the present owner

Part of a set of four surviving pieces
(see cat. nos. 11 & 12)

Lent by William Hughlett Naylor

These window seats, a pier table (cat. no. 12)
and card table (cat. no. 11) are the only known
pieces of what must have been a larger set of
painted Baltimore furniture. However, other
pieces from this set may still be owned by
descendants of the Macgill family in Georgia.

These window or "recess seats," as they are
referred to in numerous newspaper advertisements of Hugh and John Finlay, appear not to
have been made to fit a specific window opening
as the Buchanan window seat (cat. no. 7). Its
length was probably a standard one, conforming
to an established window measurement in
Baltimore townhouses of the early 19th century.

The bowed-front seat rail is decorated with a
succession of gilt-framed, rectangular panels and
gilt paterae on a black background. Gilt rosettes
appear on the stiles of each front leg. The
striping of the front legs and the cuffs at the
termination of each leg are in the typical manner
of the Finlays. The end supports of this piece,
though somewhat reduced in scale, repeat the
turnings and basic design of the backs of the
chairs and settees in the set of Morris furniture
made by the brothers Finlay (cat. nos. 3 & 4).
In both instances, the vertical supports of the
back form lancet arches. In a Finlay newspaper
advertisement of 1803 (repro. in the listing of
cabinetmakers), there is an illustration of a
chair which repeats this same form. On the top
rail of each end support of these window or
recess seats, sawtooth-edged, gilt rectangles flank
the polygonal, polychrome paintings of musical
instruments.

11 CARD TABLE ca. 1800-10

Attributed to Hugh and John Finlay

Wood painted black with gilt and polychrome decoration

Height: 29½ in.; width: 35⅞ in.; depth: 17¾ in.

Provenance: Macgill family of Shepherdstown, West Virginia; by descent to the present owner

Part of a set of four surviving pieces (see cat. nos. 10 & 12)

Lent by William Hughlett Naylor

This square card table with ovolo corners repeats the quality of design and decorative detail found in its matching window seats and pier table (cat. nos. 10 & 12), and the decorative devices used are associated with the workmanship of the Finlays. In the central panel of the skirt is a polychrome painting of musical instruments on a floral background. This is flanked by rectangular, sawtooth-edged, gilt panels which are repeated at each end and on the ovolo corners of the skirt. Paterae in two tones of gilt occur on the stiles of each of the four legs, and there is a stylized grape vine motif on the edges of the table top, very similar in execution to the same decorative motif on the Morris set of Finlay furniture (cat. nos. 3-5).

Underneath the table top, there is a medial cross brace typical of Baltimore card tables of the period, and one of the rear legs is hinged to support the top when open.

12   PIER TABLE ca. 1800-10

Attributed to Hugh and John Finlay

Wood painted black with gilt and polychrome decoration

Height: 36 in.; width: 34⅞ in.; depth: 20⅛ in.

Provenance: Macgill family of Shepherdstown, West Virginia; by descent to the present owner

Part of a set of four surviving pieces (see cat. nos. 10 & 11)

Private Collection

The forms of the curvilinear cupid's-bow front apron and the concave-shaped side panels of this pier table are repeated in the shaping of the top. This same form is seen in a pier table (cat. no. 16) and further relates these two tables to the two marble-topped corner tables with *verre églomisé* panels (cat. nos. 1 & 2). The design of the sawtooth-edged, gilt ornament on each panel at the end skirts and on the front skirt flanking the painting of musical instruments is identical to the decoration on the set of painted furniture made for the Buchanan family (cat. nos. 6-9). The striping on the legs, typical of Baltimore painted furniture of this period, relates closely to the striping on the Finlay set made for John Morris (cat. nos. 3-5) as well as the Buchanan set. Of special interest is the block cuff near the termination of each of four legs. They are set at angles to conform to the shaping of the top. The same arrangement is also evident in the block cuffing on the two marble-topped corner tables (cat. nos. 1 & 2). Gilt rosettes appear on two sides of the block cuffs of the front legs and on one side of the rear legs. There is also a banded, lozenge-shaped, acanthus leaf decoration on the stile of each of the four legs, similar to that on the corner tables (mentioned above) and a pier table (cat. no. 16).

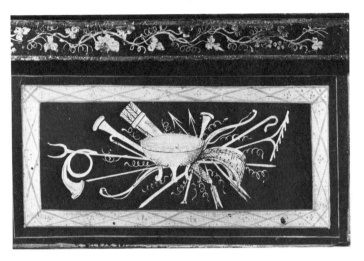

13 CARD TABLE ca. 1800-10

Possible attribution to Hugh and John Finlay

Wood painted black with gilt decoration; baize playing surface

Height: 29⅝ in.; width: 36⅛ in.; depth: 17⅝ in.

Provenance: Robert Gilmor, II; Samuel Riggs of Baltimore, business partner of George Peabody (purchased table at a sale of effects of Robert Gilmor, II in the 1850's); Elisha Riggs of Montgomery County (brother of Samuel); by descent to the present owners

Lent by the Misses Martha Sprigg Poole and Katherine Riggs Poole

This square card table with ovolo corners is in the sophisticated style and of the quality associated with the work of Hugh and John Finlay. The five painted panels of musical, armorial and agricultural trophies are similar to those on other examples of known Finlay furniture as is the use of gold, diaper-banded panels, enframing rectangular-shaped vine and leaf designs (see cat. no. 5).

The bow, arrow and quiver design on the stiles of each leg are nearly identical to those on the pier table made for John Morris (cat. no. 5). The grapevine motif, occurring in this example on each of the front legs and the edges of the table top, is also found on the Morris set.

14   CARD TABLE ca. 1800-10

Possible attribution to Hugh and John Finlay

Wood painted black with gilt and polychrome decoration

Height: 29⅝ in.; width: 35⅞ in.; depth: 17⅝ in.

Provenance: Maynadier and Key families of Anne Arundel County; acquired by present owner from descendant of the Maynadier family

Part of a set of two surviving pieces (see cat. no. 15)

Lent by The National Society of the
Colonial Dames of America in the State of Maryland

The predominant decoration of this square card table with ovolo corners is the polychrome architectural view at the center of the skirt. The building depicted is *Mount Clare*, a house begun by Charles Carroll, the Barrister, near Baltimore about 1760. This view is nearly identical to and most certainly by the hand of the same ornamenter as another rendering of *Mount Clare* on the back of one of the settees in the Morris set of furniture made by the Finlays (cat. no. 4). There is no known connection between the Maynadier, Key and Charles Carroll families to suggest any personal reason for the original owners to purchase a card table decorated with a view of *Mount Clare*.

The architectural view of this card table is flanked by gilt, scrollwork decoration derived from designs by Thomas Sheraton. This same decoration appears on each end of the skirt. On the ovolo corners of the skirt there is gilt patera decoration which also appears on the stile of each leg. Gold striping and a leaf and vine motif are found on the front of each of the four legs and stylized-diapering in gilt appears on the edges of the table top. Two side chairs (cat. no. 18) employ identical elements of decoration but have a different history of ownership. The cuffed bottoms of the legs are also typical of Baltimore painted furniture of this period.

The construction details of the cross bracing, beneath the top of the table and the hinging of the rear legs follow the typical pattern of Baltimore card tables.

15 SIDE TABLE ca. 1800-10

Possible attribution to Hugh and John Finlay

Wood painted black with gilt and polychrome decoration

Height: 29½ in.; width: 42⅛ in.; depth: 19⅞ in.

Provenance: The Key and Maynadier families of Anne Arundel County; by descent to present owners

Part of a set of two surviving pieces (see cat. no. 14)

Lent by Mr. and Mrs. William M. Maynadier

This table has the same provenance as the card table (cat. no. 14) and was also used at a house called *Belvoir,* owned successively by the Maynadier and Key families of Anne Arundel County. The same basic elements of polychrome and gilt decoration are repeated — an architectural view on the center of the skirt flanked by gilt scroll decoration and paterae, a stylized-diapering of the edges of the top, and paterae on the stiles of each leg. The presence in both examples of an architectural view suggests the shop of the Finlays or at least the work of the same ornamenter, although the other decorations employed are not up to the quality of their shop standards.

The brass casters applied to each of the four legs would seem to be of later 19th-century date. Most likely, the legs of this side table were originally the same as those on its matching card table with cuffs at the bottom. These were probably removed to make the table shorter or to apply the brass casters.

The house depicted in the architectural view has not as yet been identified.

16   **PIER TABLE** ca. 1810-20

Possible attribution to Hugh and John Finlay

Wood grained to simulate rosewood with gilt
decoration; white marble top

Height: 31⅞ in.; width: 44⅛ in.; depth: 21¾ in.

Provenance: John B. Morris of *Clermont* (near
Baltimore); given to the Museum by descendant

The Baltimore Museum of Art
Gift of Lydia Howard de Roth in memory of
her sister, Nancy H. De Ford Venable   69.23.1

39

The form of the unusual serpentine or cupid's-
bow front of this pier table is repeated in the
shaped, white marble top and is related to earlier
nineteenth-century Baltimore furniture believed
to have been produced in the shop of the Finlays
(see cat. no. 12). In the center of the apron is a
painted gilt design of musical instruments
flanked on each side by Grecian scrolls,
anthemion, and vine and tendril motifs. The
design for the decoration on these two flanking
panels, repeated on the two ends of the apron,
is Classical Revival in source rather than
Adamesque. The legs are striped to simulate
inlay or reeding, and on the stile of each leg,
painted in gilt, is a motif of banded acanthus
leaves (see cat. nos. 1, 2 & 12).

17   CARD TABLE ca. 1810-20

Wood painted black with gilt and polychrome
decoration; mahogany top with painted playing
surface

Height: 29⅝ in.; width: 36⅛ in.; depth: 17¾ in.

Provenance: Joseph Kindig, Jr.

The Baltimore Museum of Art
Philip B. Perlman Fund   60.45

This card table has an intricately-shaped top and
apron. A romantic landscape scene is painted on
the center of the apron flanked by rectangular
panels formed by gilt acanthus leaves, a design
repeated on the end skirts. Less elaborate, gilt
panels are on the concave corners of the skirt or
apron. There is an entwined leaf design on each
of the four legs which have protruding cuffs near
their terminations in the Baltimore manner. The
top leaf is of mahogany but when opened the
playing surface is painted black with gilt-striped
borders and a gilt floral and diamond design at
each of the concave corners.

18 SIDE CHAIR (One of two) ca. 1810

Possible attribution to Hugh and John Finlay

Wood painted black with polychrome and gilt decoration

Height: 34½ in.; width: 17½ in.; depth: 15¾ in.

Provenance: Birckhead and Van Deventer families of Baltimore; purchased by the Museum from descendant

Part of a set of three surviving pieces; settee, private collection (not included here)

The Baltimore Museum of Art
Middendorf Fund   72.23.1 & 2

The crest rails of each of the two chair backs contain a polychrome architectural view of a country house: one cannot be identified; the other is *Greenwood*, built in the environs of Baltimore circa 1800 by Philip Rogers. The rendering of *Greenwood* is nearly identical to that of the same building that appears on the pier table in the Morris set of Finlay furniture (cat. no. 5). This would suggest a possible attribution to the Finlays' shop even though the quality of decoration is not up to their standards. By the similarity of decoration, it can be assumed that these chairs have been decorated by the same ornamenter as the card and side table from the Maynadier and Key families (cat. nos. 14 & 15). Identical gilt scrolls in the style of Sheraton flank each architectural view. There is also the repeated use of gilt paterae and diapering as well as similar gilt striping on the back supports and legs of the chairs.

The unusual arrangement of the half or split spindles as vertical members of the chair back does not occur on other known examples of Baltimore painted furniture. The rush bottom seats appear to be original and, although not commonplace in Baltimore chairs of the period, they are mentioned in the advertisements of the Finlays and other cabinetmakers.

There is additional gilt decoration in the form of rosettes on the stiles of each front leg as well as rosettes and a spear motif on the front stretcher. The front legs are striped in gilt and terminate in spade feet in the typical manner of chair and table legs of Baltimore painted furniture of the early 19th century.

19 **SIDE CHAIR** (One of a pair) ca. 1815
Thomas S. Renshaw, cabinetmaker
John Barnhart, ornamenter

Wood painted a putty color with gilt and polychrome decoration

Height: 34¾ in.; width: 19 in.; depth: 16 in.

Provenance: Collection, Mrs. Rush Sturges

Part of a set of three surviving pieces (see cat. no. 20)

The Baltimore Museum of Art
Gift of Friends of the Museum   50.52 a & b

20 **SETTEE** ca. 1815
Thomas S. Renshaw, cabinetmaker
John Barnhart, ornamenter

Wood painted a putty color with gilt and polychrome decoration

Height: 35¼ in.; length: 76½ in.; depth: 20⅝ in.

Provenance: Collection, Mrs. Rush Sturges

Part of a set of three surviving pieces (see cat. no. 19)

The Baltimore Museum of Art
Gift of Friends of the Museum   50.51

Inscribed on the back of the seat rail of the settee are the names Thomas S. Renshaw and John Barnhart. In the Baltimore City Directories for the period 1800-40, the name Thomas Renshaw appears only once for a two year period (1814-15) at the address, 37 South Gay Street. For this same time period, the name John Barnhart appears four times in the City Directories — twice (1822-23, 1824) as a letterer and sign painter, once as a letterer (1827), and later (1829) as an ornamental painter. Since much painted furniture with Maryland provenances has survived that can stylistically be attributed to Renshaw, it would appear that he worked for many years in Baltimore, indicating that the information obtained from the City Directories does not always provide a complete record.

It is interesting to note that according to the City Directories, the address for the cabinetmaking shop at 37 South Gay Street, in the center of Baltimore's cabinetmaking industry, was occupied by the Baltimore cabinetmaker Robert Fisher (City Directory listing, 1804, 1807 & 1810; see discussion of Robert Fisher, cat. no. 6); Lachlan Phyfe, the brother of Duncan Phyfe of New York and said in later years to be his best carver (City Directory listing, 1807 & 1808) and later by Thomas S. Renshaw.

The putty-colored ground of this pair of chairs and the settee is enhanced by gilt and polychrome decoration. On the chair backs and on the back of the settee are painted scenes of fanciful and romantic design. While these two chairs and the settee are, by the signature of Renshaw and Barnhart, the only such documented pieces of Baltimore painted furniture, they do not represent its highest achievements.

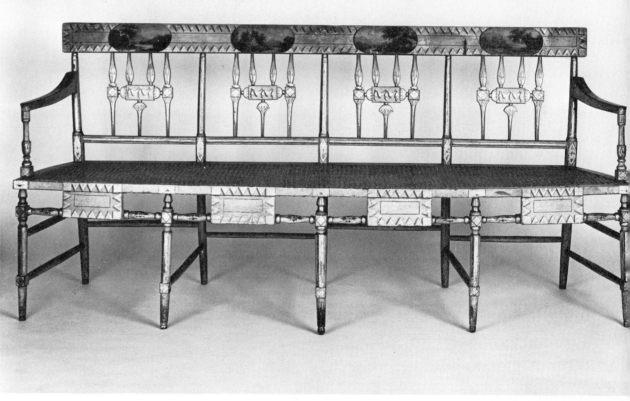

21   **SIDE CHAIR** (One of four) ca. 1815
Attributed to Thomas S. Renshaw, cabinetmaker
John Barnhart, ornamenter

Wood painted red with gilt and polychrome
decoration

Height: 35⅜ in.; width: 18¾ in.; depth: 15⅞ in.

The Baltimore Museum of Art
Philip B. Perlman Fund   70.29 a-d

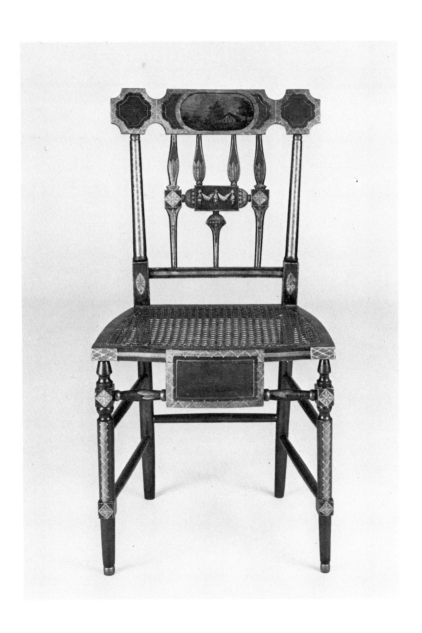

With the exception of the crest rail, the turnings
and decoration on the chair back are nearly identical to those on the settee, signed by Thomas S.
Renshaw and John Barnhart, and its matching
side chairs (cat. nos. 19 & 20), as are the turnings
of the front legs, arrangement of the stretchers,
and the use of a decorated apron below the front
seat rail. The painted landscape panel is again
fanciful.

The unusually-shaped crest rail is closely related
to a chair in the Winterthur Museum (Montgomery, p. 450-51, repro., p. 450).

There has been some restoration of the gilt
decoration and landscape panels on each of
these four chairs.

22   SIDE CHAIR (One of three) ca. 1820

Wood painted red with polychrome, stenciled and freehand gilt decoration

Height: 33⅜ in.; width: 18⅛ in.; depth: 15⅞ in.

Lent by The Maryland Historical Society
Gift of Mrs. Charles Webb

Although mentioned in numerous advertisements of the Finlays and other early 19th-century cabinetmakers, rush seats are not common in surviving Baltimore painted furniture. Caning rather than rushing may have been considered more elegant for the bottom of chairs and settees and therefore thought to be best suited to the high quality of Baltimore painted furniture.

The large panel of the crest rail is decorated with gilt striping and a key design and with a romantic landscape similar to those employed on the painted furniture made by Thomas Renshaw and ornamented by John Barnhart (see cat. nos. 19-21). There is gilt striping on the turned supports and X-shaped back. The turned front legs are similarly striped, and a gilt armorial trophy is found on the front stretcher.

23   SIDE CHAIR (One of three) ca. 1820

Wood painted black with polychrome and gilt decoration

Height: 32⅜ in.; width: 17¾ in.; depth: 15¾ in.

Provenance: John B. Morris family of *Clermont,* Baltimore; given to the Museum by descendant

The Baltimore Museum of Art
Gift of Lydia Howard de Roth
in memory of Nancy H. De Ford Venable   69.23.2-4

The design of this side chair has been derived from the Sheraton fancy chair tradition, so popularized and perpetuated in painted rush bottom chairs of other American cabinetmaking centers during the same period when higher quality painted furniture was being produced in Baltimore by the Finlays and others. A polychrome leaf painting is found on the small block inset between the two horizontal members forming the crest rail. The three spindles of the back are decorated with leaf designs in gilt and glazes. On the center spindle is a similarly executed leaf design at the top section of its icicle shape. The stiles as well as the front legs with their cuffed bottoms are typical of Baltimore furniture of this period. Gilt decoration is also found on the front stretcher.

24 SIDE CHAIR (One of two) ca. 1820-30

Wood painted black with gilt decoration; brass mountings

Height: 30⅝ in.; width: 18⅛ in.; depth: 16½ in.

Provenance: Wilson family of Baltimore; by descent to the present owners

Lent by Mr. and Mrs. James I. Randall

The design for this side chair, called in Baltimore a "wheelback" chair, appears to be based on a Roman camp chair which had a hinge to allow the folding of the back and rear legs — a feature obviously not duplicated here. The front legs are also based on an antique, classical, Roman source as is the form of the side rails of the seat. The ring turnings at the top of each of the four legs and at the base of the back supports were common design features employed by Baltimore cabinetmakers.

The large horizontal crest rail at the back is decorated with a motif of crossed torches inset in a wreath flanked by Grecian scrolls and cornucopias related to the decoration on the skirt of a Baltimore pier table (cat. no. 42). The decoration on the smaller, stay rail and the front rail of the seat is related to that on other Baltimore painted chairs of the period (see cat. no. 37).

The caned seat lifts out, adding credence to the tradition that, in Baltimore, these chairs were manufactured with summer and winter seats.

25 WINDOW STOOL ca. 1820-30

Wood grained to simulate rosewood with gilt decoration; brass mountings

Height: 15⅝ in.; length: 45¼ in.; depth: 16¼ in.

Provenance: Wilson family of Baltimore; by descent to present owners

One of three matching stools: pair, Winterthur Museum (Montgomery, p. 315, repro., p. 314)

Part of a group of eight pieces (see cat. nos. 26-31 and Miller, I, pp. 319-20; repro., p. 321)

Lent by Mr. and Mrs. J. Hollis Albert, Jr.

Of the eight pieces which were presumably purchased as a related group and were part of the furnishings of a Baltimore house called *Hunington* and later used at *Stoneleigh,* five pieces could be accurately called part of a matching set (see cat. nos. 27-31). Of the remaining three pieces, this window stool, a sofa (Miller, I, pp. 319-20, repro. p. 321), and a couch with scroll ends (cat. no. 26) have matching gilt decoration. The chairs (cat. no. 24) traditionally used with these furnishings, though typical of Baltimore painted furniture of the early 19th century, do not match in design or decoration any of the other pieces. From surviving evidence, it would appear that matching chairs were not always provided with sets of painted furniture but often bought from existing stock items.

Anthemion motifs appear on the Greek antifixes at the corner of the seat and on the front of each of the four legs. Of the gilt decoration employed on this window stool, the ornamental design of the seat rail relates most closely to the decoration of the scroll-end couch (cat. no. 26).

26 COUCH ca. 1820-30

Wood grained to simulate rosewood with gilt decoration; brass mountings

Height: 25 in.; length: 66¼ in.; depth: 20 in.

Provenance: Wilson family of Baltimore; by descent to the present owners

Part of a group of eight pieces (see cat. nos. 25, 27-31 and Miller, I pp. 319-20; repro., p. 321)

Lent by Mr. and Mrs. Hugh Benet, Jr.

49

Acanthus leaf and anthemion decoration is found on the curved, cornucopia-shaped legs of this couch. The gilt brass, dolphin casters are also found on a card table of this period (cat. no. 41). On the simulated rosewood graining of the seat rail and scroll ends, there is applied gilt decoration derived from classical sources.

With the exception of the decoration on the central section of the seat rail and a slight variation in size, this couch is identical to one in the Winterthur Museum (Montgomery, pp. 313-315; repro., p. 314). A pair of similar couches of greater length, originally owned by the Bonaparte family of Baltimore, are now in the collection at *Hampton* near Baltimore.

27 MIXING TABLE ca. 1820-30

Wood grained to simulate rosewood with stenciled and freehand gilt decoration; white marble top and brass mountings

Height: 38½ in.; width: 33 in.; depth: 18½ in.

Provenance: Wilson family of Baltimore; by descent to present owners

Part of a group of eight pieces (see cat. nos. 25, 26, 28-31 and Miller, I, pp. 319-20; repro., p. 321)

Lent by Mr. and Mrs. John M. Myers

This marble-topped mixing table of unusual height is supported on an X-frame, pedestal base similar to those on the other tables owned by the Wilson family of Baltimore (cat. nos. 28-30), and the classically-derived, stenciled and freehand gilt decoration is closely related to that on the entire group (cat. nos. 25, 26 & 28-31).

On the front and each end of the skirt there is a repetitive, Grecian scroll design in gilt. The turned hub of the pedestal base is decorated with five brass rosettes which do not encircle the base as the table was intended to stand against a wall. On the front of each of the scroll supports, there are similar brass rosettes from which spring Grecian scroll and anthemion designs in gilt with the motif of a winged thunderbolt underneath on the X-frame base. The front side of each of the four saber legs is decorated with a gilt acanthus leaf design, and the legs terminate in brass, animal paw mountings with casters. On each end of the X-frame base, there is an encircled, fanlike anthemion design. A classical rosette and leaf design decorates the front of the pedestal base. Gilt striping outlines most of the structural members.

28 PIER TABLE ca. 1820-30

Wood grained to simulate rosewood with stenciled and freehand gilt decoration; marble top and brass mountings

Height: 36⅜ in.; width: 46¼ in.; depth: 22¼ in.

Provenance: Wilson family of Baltimore; by descent to the present owners

Part of a group of eight pieces (see cat. nos. 25-27, 29-31 and Miller, I, pp. 319-20; repro., p. 321)

Lent by Mr. and Mrs. Edgar Nash, III

This pier table employs the same elements of design and decoration as the mixing table (cat. no. 27) and the pair of circular tables (cat. nos. 29 & 30) from the set of painted furniture made for the Wilson family of Baltimore. The decoration on the front and end skirts of the table are essentially an anthemion and acanthus leaf design, flanked by Grecian scrolls. The hub of the pedestal base is enriched with applied brass rosettes; on the X-stretcher base and scroll supports, there are gilt acanthus leaf, anthemion and winged thunderbolt designs. The table is mounted on four brass, animal paw feet with casters.

29 CENTER TABLE ca. 1820-30

Wood grained to simulate rosewood with polychrome, stenciled and freehand gilt decoration; painted slate top and brass mountings

Height: 30¼ in.; diameter of the top: 33⅛ in.

Provenance: Wilson family of Baltimore; by descent to the present owners

One of a matching pair; mate, private collection (see cat. no. 30)

One of a group of eight pieces (see cat. nos. 25-28, 30, 31 and Miller, I, pp. 319-20; repro., p. 321)

Lent by Mr. and Mrs. John M. Myers

With the exception of the decoration on the skirt and the subject matter of the enameled and painted top, this circular table is identical to a matching one, also originally owned by the Wilson family of Baltimore (cat. no. 30). The turned, pedestal support, set on an X-frame base with saber legs, is closely related to those on the pier table and mixing table from this same group of painted furniture (cat. nos. 27 & 28). Brass rosettes decorate the hub of the pedestal support. The wide variety of decorative devices in gilt associated with this group of furniture are repeated on the base — brass rosettes on the scroll supports, gilt acanthus leaves, anthemia and the design of a winged thunderbolt. The skirt of the table is decorated with a central anthemion motif flanked by acanthus leaf Grecian scrolls — the same design which is on the skirt of the pier table and mixing table from this same group.

Slate tops covered with plaster and painted with enamels were often called "Italian tops" and would appear to be of European import as they are found on examples of painted furniture from Philadelphia and elsewhere. The very beautifully executed scene here is of figures set on a rocky coastline with a sailing vessel in the background. Inscribed in chalk on the underside of this top are the words *Maritime Vernet* which may refer to either Claude Joseph Vernet or Carle Vernet. Such maritime paintings were typical of the work of Claude Vernet who was born in Avignon in 1714 and died in Paris in 1789, and he is known for a set of twenty paintings of French seaports as well as numerous landscapes and romantic classic ruins, the subject matter for the enameled top of the matching center table of this group. Carle Vernet was born in Bordeaux in 1758 and lived until 1836. Numerous early 19th-century engravings survive after his paintings of maritime romantic scenes. These painted tops on the center tables were, most likely, the performance of a competent artist based on the engraved works of one of the Vernets.

On each top, the paintings are framed in a circular border of gilt beading outside of which there is a gilt wreath of acorn and oak leaves. This latter design could well have been based on a French design for plaster in such works as Josèphe Beunat (no. 409, plate 2).

53

30 CENTER TABLE ca. 1820-30

Wood grained to simulate rosewood with polychrome, stenciled and freehand gilt decoration, and freehand bronzing; painted slate top and brass mountings

Height: 29¾ in.; diameter of top: 32⅝ in.

Provenance: Wilson family of Baltimore; by descent to the present owner

One of a matching pair; mate, private collection (see cat. no. 29)

Part of a group of eight pieces (see cat. nos. 25-29, 31 and Miller, I, pp. 319-20; repro., p. 321)

Lent by Mrs. William M. Poultney

The pedestal base and X-frame support of this center table is identical to the preceding one (cat. no. 29). However, there is mounted under the pedestal base, for decoration rather than strength, a lacquered brass ring which would have also been found on the other circular table but was removed or lost many years ago.

Instead of a repeated anthemion and Greek scroll design on the skirt of the table, there is a polychrome, stenciled design of fruit and foliage. A gilt band is found at the top and bottom of this motif. Painted in enamels on the plaster-covered top is a scene of a ruined Greco-Roman temple set in a romantic landscape. The painting is encircled by gilt beading and an oak leaf and acorn design identical to that on its matching circular table.

31   LAMP STAND ca. 1820-30

Wood grained to simulate rosewood with stenciled polychrome, stenciled and freehand gilt decoration, and freehand bronzing; brass mountings

Height: 62⅜ in.

Provenance: Wilson family of Baltimore; by descent to the present owner

Part of a group of eight pieces (see cat. nos. 25-30 and Miller, I, pp. 319-20; repro., p. 321)

Lent by Mrs. William D. Poultney

This grained and decorated lamp or candle stand was used with the other pieces of Wilson family furniture (cat. nos. 25-30) and repeats many of their decorative devices. The shaft or column of this lamp stand is believed to have been turned from a readily-available stock piece of 4 x 4 lumber. A close examination of the turnings of the torus moldings at the bottom of the column, in the center and of the top support reveals what appears to be inset pieces of wood that actually were applied before turning to the areas where a greater width was desired. At the top of the lamp stand, there is gilt acanthus leaf decoration which is repeated on the column near the base. Near the center of the column, there is a bulbous turning decorated with a stenciled fruit and foliage motif in polychromy with freehand bronzing. The scroll base supports are enriched with gilt scrolls and brass rosettes and relate to other pedestal-based pieces in the Wilson family furniture (see cat. nos. 27-30).

32 SOFA ca. 1820-30

Mahogany with stenciled and freehand gilt decoration
Height: 35 in.; width: 90⅝ in.; depth: 23¾ in.
Provenance: Waters family of *Beechwood*, Princess
Anne, Somerset County, Maryland; by descent to
present owners
Lent by Mr. and Mrs. Henry W. Keating

The exposed mahogany members of this scroll-
end sofa have been decorated with freehand and
stenciled gilt decoration. The crest rail of the
curvilinear back is edged with a gilt acanthus
leaf design and, at its center, is a rectangular-
shaped, gilt-edged plaque surrounding an
armorial motif flanked by floral sprays. These
sprays are repeated on the mahogany scroll ends
which terminate in a rosette. On the exposed
front of the seat rail is the applied gilt
decoration of a double-pointed spear, on the
center of which is imposed an acanthus leaf
wreath. A motif of small armorial trophies is
found on the seat rail above each scroll foot.
These feet are edged with a gilt acanthus leaf
design and gilt rosettes are found at their
terminations.

The basic form of this sofa is typical of examples
produced in other major east coast cabinetmaking centers, but the applied gilt decoration
is in the Baltimore painted furniture tradition.

57

58

33   SIDE CHAIR ca. 1820-30
Mahogany with gilt decoration
Height: 32⅞ in.; width: 16½ in.; depth: 16¼ in.
The Baltimore Museum of Art
Philip B. Perlman Fund   66.12

This saber-legged side chair is derived from the
Greek klismos form. The gilt decoration on the
tablet of the turned crest rail forms a vase and
plumed design. On the shaped back rail, there
is a rosette and palmette design. Thick gilt
stripes run in continuous lines from the top of
the back down to the foot of each front leg.
Fanlike palmettes occur on the side of the seat
rails above the front saber legs. The sides of all
four legs are outlined in gilt.

34 BENCH OR SETTEE ca. 1820-30

Wood painted black with stenciled polychrome, stenciled and freehand gilt decoration and freehand bronzing; brass mountings

Height: 27¼ in.; length: 92½ in.; depth: 20¾ in.

The Baltimore Museum of Art
Museum Purchase 64.49

This cane-seated bench or settee in what can be called the archeological, classical style is mounted on four turned legs with the front legs reeded as well. At the top of each front leg, there is a trophy motif in gilt. There are mounted, wooden, cylindrical and upholstered arms or headrests at each end, imitative of Roman couches or beds. On the front of the convex seat rail there is a stenciled polychrome design with freehand bronzing which is related to a similar design of fruit and foliage on a circular table (cat. no. 30). The apricot-colored, wool upholstery at each end is original and contains fanlike anthemion designs.

The design source for this bench would most likely be Thomas Hope's *Household Furniture and Interior Decoration . . .* or Percier and Fontaine's *Recueil de Décorations Intérieures. . . .* The design is also strongly related to the pair of settees or window benches believed to have been made by the Finlays after designs by Benjamin H. Latrobe for the White House during the Madison administration but were destroyed in the conflagration of 1814.

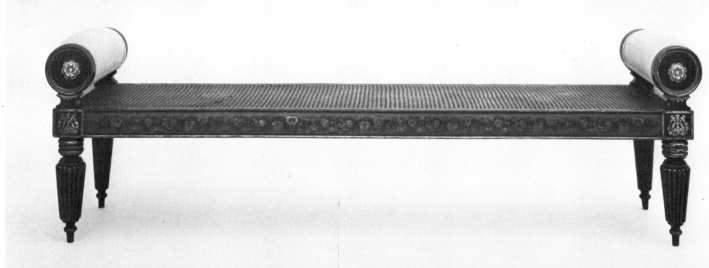

Wood painted black and wood grained to simulate rosewood with stenciled and freehand gilt decoration; metal monopodic supports; marble top and mirror back

Height: 37¼ in.; width: 45⅝ in.; depth: 22¼ in.

Provenance: Hoffman family of Baltimore; bequeathed to the Museum by descendant

The Baltimore Museum of Art
The Hanson Rawlings Duval, Jr.
Memorial Collection, Bequest of
Elizabeth Curzon Hoffman Wing   67.30.13

The two monopodic, metal supports or trapezophorons appear to have been copied from a direct classical source. The back supports framing the mirror are grained to simulate rosewood. On each side of the mirror there is a gilt leaf, flower and vase motif. It would actually appear that this stenciled and freehand gilt decoration was applied upside down. Below the mirror in gilt there is a spray of acorns and oak leaves. The skirt of the table beneath the white marble top is a combination of gilded plaster and ormolu decoration in the form of an anthemion frieze, again derived from a direct classical source. In fact, this frieze, in design, is very similar to that found on the architrave of the doorway in the north porch of the Erechtheum (Lawrence, fig. 97, p. 167).

The brass mountings on the skirt of the table at the top of each monopodic support are replacements.

According to family tradition this pier table was part of the original furnishings of the house designed by Robert Mills, ca. 1817, for a member of the Hoffman family of Baltimore.

36   CHAIR (One of nine) ca. 1820-30

Wood painted yellow with polychrome, stenciled and freehand gilt decoration

Height: 33⅞ in.; width: 17¾ in.; depth: 16¼ in.

Provenance: Abell family of Baltimore, originally used in a house called *Woodbourne*

Part of a set of eleven surviving chairs; two, descendants of the Abell family

Lent by The Metropolitan Museum of Art Purchase, Mrs. Paul Moore Gift

Of all known Baltimore chairs in the classical, archaeological style, these side chairs, which must have originally numbered an even dozen, achieve the true Greco-Roman klismos form more than any other. This is especially evident in the graceful shape of the raked back and curvilinear crest rail. On each broad crest rail, superimposed on a field of black-green, there is a different motif of either griffins, unicorns or other mythological animals, all flanked by Grecian scrolls. This decoration is undoubtedly derived from plate 56 of Thomas Sheraton's *The Cabinet-maker and Upholsterer's Drawing-Book* (1802 edition). Nearly identical designs appear on the backs of the chairs and other pieces in the Alexander Brown set of furniture (cat. nos. 49-52). They are most likely by the same hand, but there has unfortunately been some repainting on the Alexander Brown chairs that thickens the linear quality of the original design. In this chair on the smaller stay rail, there is a design of a horizontally-imposed eagle standard at the center of which is a laurel wreath criss-crossed with torches. On the front seat rail, there is a design, in polychrome glazes, of bound fasces flanked by a wreath and medallion design in black-green. On the side rails above the front and back legs, there is the repeated motif of a winged thunderbolt as well as fanlike palmettes or anthemion designs connected by a linear, diamond pattern. The turned front legs have inset cuffs and are decorated below the top turnings with fan palmettes and drapery swags. The striping on the rear saber legs is closely related to that on the rear legs of the Alexander Brown chairs.

37   SIDE CHAIR ca. 1820-30

Wood grained to simulate rosewood with stenciled
and freehand gilt decoration
Height: 30½ in.; width: 18 in.; depth: 15¾ in.
Private Collection

This side chair retains most of its original
decoration and appears to have never been
restored or repainted. The broad crest rail
of the back is banded in gold and contains a
central motif of a gilt, fanlike anthemion
flanked by cornucopias, Grecian scrolls, and, at
each end, a repetition of the anthemion design.
The decoration on the stay rail is identical to
that employed on three sides of the top surface
of a card table (cat. no. 41). The bottom section
of this chair, with its elbow-shaped side rails,
turned front legs and front stretcher, is of
identical design to a pair of window seats that
were part of the 19th-century furnishings of the
Moses Myers House in Norfolk (cat. no. 38).
Obviously this chair and the window seat are
from the same shop, and the gilt decoration on
simulated rosewood is the work of the same
chair ornamenter. Linear, scroll and palmette
leaf designs decorate the sides of the elbow-
shaped back supports, and coupled, gilt rosettes
appear on the side rails above the front legs. The
decoration on the front stretcher is also identical
to that on the stretchers connecting the three
front legs of the window seats from the Moses
Myers House.

Below layers of later upholstery the original,
scarlet wool seat covering was found intact. The
stamped pomegranate design can still be seen in
this somewhat faded fabric.

38   WINDOW SEAT (One of a pair) ca. 1820-30

Wood grained to simulate rosewood with painted
gilt decoration

Height: 20⅛ in.; length: 50½ in.; depth: 17½ in.

Provenance: Moses Myers of Norfolk

Lent by the Moses Myers House of
The Chrysler Museum, Norfolk

These window seats, part of the early 19th-
century furnishings of the Moses Myers House in
Norfolk, have always been used in the first floor
parlor. In the Moses Myers inventory of 1820,
mention is made of two seats or "rupees" which
may be a reference to this pair.

In design, these window seats are exactly like the
lower half of a Baltimore painted chair of the
period (cat. no. 37). The elbow shapes of the
side rails and their decoration are identical, as
are the turnings of the three front legs and the
gilt decoration on the stretchers joining them.

Close communication by sail and steam packet
in the first decades of the 19th century could
explain the presence of Baltimore furniture in
Norfolk.

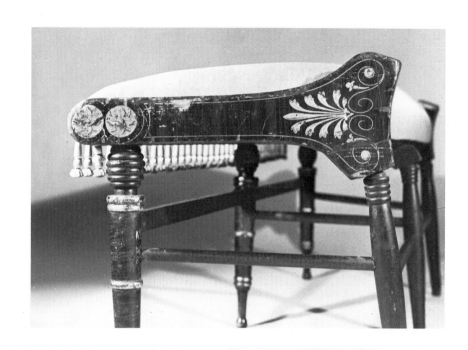

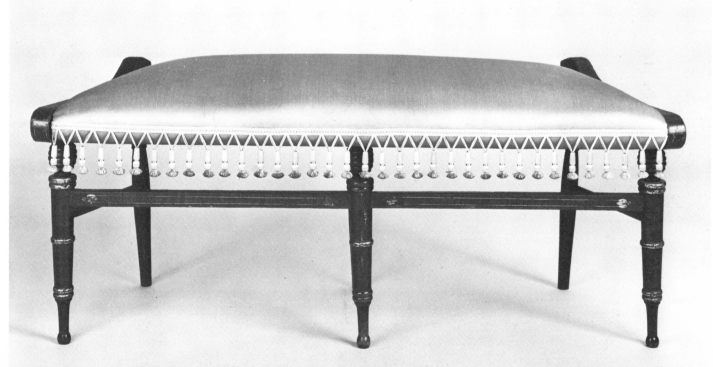

39 SIDE CHAIR ca. 1820-30

Wood painted black with stenciled and freehand gilt decoration

Height: 32⅛ in.; width: 17¾ in.; depth: 16⅛ in.

Lent by Mr. and Mrs. Thomas T. Fell

The design of this side chair is based on that of an ancient Roman folding chair. At the juncture of the side rails and the back supports, there are wedge or elbow-shaped members rather than the usual Baltimore wheel-shaped turnings (see cat. no. 24). The ring turnings at the top of the reeded front legs and turned rear legs, and those at the base of the back supports, are seen on other examples of Baltimore painted side chairs (see cat. no. 37). The ample crest rail is banded in gilt and contains a stenciled decoration of a bowl of classical shape, flanked by cornucopias. These cornucopias are also repeated in the gilt design on the smaller stay rail. Though much of the gilt decoration of this side chair has been worn away through use, the original design can easily be visually reconstructed. It is of interest to note that the ends of the cornucopias are actually birds' or eagles' heads. Acanthus leaf, scroll and rosette designs appear on the side elbow members, and an anthemion design appears on the front of each side rail. There is further gilt decoration in the form of the striping and some of the turnings on the legs and stretchers are gilded.

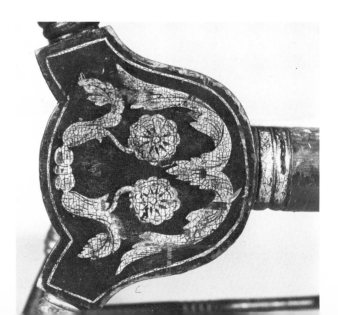

40 SIDE CHAIR ca. 1820-30

Wood grained to simulate rosewood with stenciled
and freehand gilt decoration

Height: 31⅜ in.; width: 17¼ in.; depth: 16½ in.

Lent by Mr. and Mrs. William M. Hanna

This side chair with its excellently preserved
freehand and stenciled gilt decoration represents
a type of plank bottom chair produced in great
numbers in Baltimore from the first decades of
the 19th century up to the time of the Civil War.

The grained, crest rail has a decorative motif of
a central six-pointed star and laurel wreath
flanked by cornucopias and laurel sprays. A wide
gilt band and smaller gilt stripe outline the crest
rail and are repeated on the front of the curvilinear back supports. On the sides of the
solid, plank seat, there is gilt striping and
rosettes. The two front legs with bulbous
turnings, decorated with a stylized motif in gilt,
relate more closely to Egyptian than to classic
Greco-Roman origins. On the front stretcher gilt
decoration is found in the form of a band of
laurel leaves.

Such solid plank bottom seats were often covered
with a cushion or by a thin layer of upholstery.

41 CARD TABLE ca. 1820-30

Wood grained to simulate rosewood with stenciled
polychrome, stenciled and freehand gilt decoration
and freehand bronzing; brass mountings

Height: 29 in.; width: 36 in.; depth: 17⅞ in.

The Baltimore Museum of Art
George C. Jenkins Fund   69.8.4

In form and design, this card table is stylistically
related and its decoration nearly identical to the
two circular tables (cat. nos. 29 & 30), a mixing
table (cat. no. 27), and pier table (cat. no. 28)
which were all part of a group made for the
Wilson family of Baltimore.

In the front two corners on the top, when closed,
and in each corner on the playing surface, when
opened, there is a stenciled gilt decoration in
the form of a fanlike anthemion. On the edges,
there is a coupled and singular motif of
anthemia flanked by Grecian scrolls identical
to those on a side chair (cat. no. 37). In the
center of the skirt below the table top there is a
decorative panel of a stenciled polychrome
design of fruit and foliage which is enhanced by
freehand bronzing. This motif is flanked on each
side by rectangular, gilt-framed panels also
repeated on each end. On the hub of the turned,
pedestal support, there are seven applied
brass rosettes and sixteen on the scrolls of the
X-frame pedestal base. At the end of each
member of the X-frame is a fanlike anthemion
design. Stylized anthemia appear on the scrolls
of the base, and the motif of a winged thunderbolt is also found in the decoration of the base.
The sides of the four saber legs contain stylized
acanthus leaf decoration in gilt and are
terminated by brass dolphin mounts and
casters. These same casters are found on a couch
(cat. no. 26). Underneath the swivel top there
is a compartment, lined with faded red velvet.

42   PIER TABLE (One of a pair) ca. 1820-30

Wood painted black with gilt decoration; marble top and brass mountings

Height: 31½ in.; width: 42 in.; depth: 21⅛ in.

Provenance: Ridgely family of *Hampton*

Part of a group of eleven pieces (for discussion, see cat. no. 45)

Lent by Hampton National Site
National Park Service
United States Department of the Interior

This pier table corresponds in style and decoration to numerous other pieces of Baltimore painted furniture in the classical, archaeological style (see cat. nos. 25-31, 41, 44).

The heavy hub pedestal base is decorated with ormolu rosettes, and the design motif of a winged thunderbolt, as well as fanlike anthemia and acanthus leaves, are used in the decoration of the X-stretcher base. Gilt Grecian scrolls on the front and end skirts of the table flank a central design motif of a winged thunderbolt and crossed cannons. The casters have been removed from the brass feet.

43 SIDE CHAIR ca. 1824

Wood painted black with gilt and polychrome decoration

Height: 30½ in.; width: 17¾ in.; depth: 15⅜ in.

Provenance: William Patterson of Baltimore; given to the Museum by descendant

One of three matching chairs: pair, Moses Myers House of the Chrysler Museum, Norfolk

The Baltimore Museum of Art
Gift of Randolph Mordecai   25.11.1

In form, without consideration of its special decoration, this type of chair is frequently referred to as a "Southern chair" and, in some instances, as a "Southern Hitchcock." In their own time, chairs of this variety, whether actually produced in Baltimore or neighboring Washington, were, in number, among the largest produced items of American 19th-century furniture.

The turned front legs are based on an antique source. A typical Baltimore, elbow-shaped form occurs at the juncture of the side rails of the seat and the rear legs. A polychrome portrait of Lafayette, almost identical to that on the pier table from the Moses Myers House, Norfolk (cat. no. 44), is found in the center of the sturdy crest rail and is surrounded by gilt decoration in a *rinceau* form. A band of gold also outlines this crest rail. The horizontal member below contains similar decoration, though somewhat overpainted, to that in the same location on a chair of the period (cat. no. 37).

According to family tradition, this chair was used at a banquet honoring Lafayette during his visit to Baltimore in 1824. Scharf's *Chronicles of Baltimore* (p. 415) states that on Thursday, 7 October 1824, Lafayette arrived in Baltimore and that evening he dined with a committee chosen to represent the Baltimore citizenry. Traditionally, it has been said that chairs were specially made for that occasion and William Patterson and other members of the Committee were each given a chair to commemorate the event.

44   PIER TABLE ca. 1824

Wood grained to simulate rosewood with gilt and
polychrome decoration

Height: 31½ in.; width: 49⅛ in.; depth: 23¼ in.

Provenance: Moses Myers of Norfolk

Lent by the Moses Myers House of
The Chrysler Museum, Norfolk

This pier table and two matching side chairs
(identical to cat. no. 43) were part of the early
19th-century furnishings of the Moses Myers
House and were most likely part of a larger set.
A portrait or Lafayette, set in a *rinceau* of gilt
scrolls, is found in three places on the skirt of the
table. On the front skirt this design is flanked by
two gilt-outlined panels. The design of the
X-frame pedestal base and its gilt decoration is
similar to other Baltimore tables (see cat. nos.
27-31).

45 SIDE CHAIR (One of six) ca. 1820-30
Wood painted black with gilt decoration
Height: 33⅜ in.; width: 18¾ in.; depth: 17 in.
Provenance: Ridgely family of *Hampton*
Part of a group of eleven pieces (see cat. no. 42)
Lent by Hampton National Site
National Park Service
United States Department of the Interior

These six side chairs and a matching upholstered
sofa (not included here) have, since the early
19th century, been used in the parlor at
Hampton, a late 18th-century house built in
Baltimore County by the Ridgely family. The
gilt decoration of swans and palmettes applied
on the painted back splat of each chair is also
used on the sofa. The turnings in antique style
of the front legs of the chairs are repeated in the
rear legs of the sofa.

There are in the parlor at *Hampton* eleven
pieces of painted furniture in the classical,
archaeological style, representing perhaps the
remainders of three separate sets of painted
furniture or a disinterest on the part of a
member of the Ridgely family in buying a
matched set. A pair of pier tables (cat. no. 42)
are typical of Baltimore workmanship. The
remaining two pieces, each with imported,
enameled slate tops, decorated with romantic
scenes in the style of Carle Vernet (for discussion
of enameled tops, see cat. no. 29), may also be of
local origin but do not entirely comply with the
established pattern of cabinetmaking forms and
decoration in Baltimore painted furniture.

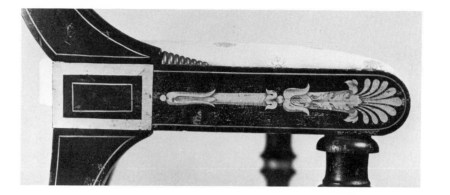

46   CARD TABLE ca. 1820-30
Wood painted yellow with polychrome, stenciled and
freehand gilt decoration
Height: 25⅝ in.; width: 36 in.; depth: 17⅞ in.
Lent by Peter Hill

The painted and stenciled design, derived from
Sheraton and found on the front skirt of this
table as well as on three sides of the top leaf
when folded, is repeated in variations on other
examples of Baltimore painted furniture (see
cat. nos. 36 & 52). This design of griffins and
Grecian leaf and anthemion scrolls is flanked
here by a motif of lyres enframed by laurel
leaves. On each end skirt, there is a central
painted panel decorated with a thunderbolt
design and a repetition of the motif of lyres and
laurel leaves at each end. A fanlike anthemion
stenciled in gilt, which is found on other
Baltimore card tables (see cat. nos. 41 & 47),
appears in two corners of the top when folded
and in each corner when opened. The table is
supported by the four turned and gilded columns
of the crossed lyre base. The curvilinear base
supports of the lyre form and the four feet,
terminating in brass mounts and casters, are
enriched with gilt acanthus leaf, anthemion and
rosette decoration.

47   CARD TABLE (One of a pair) ca. 1820-30

Wood painted yellow with polychrome decoration;
brass mountings

Height: 28⅞ in.; width: 36 in.; depth: 17¾ in.

Provenance: Patterson family of Baltimore; by
descent to present owners

Part of a set of six surviving pieces; four chairs,
private collection (see Miller, I, p. 225, repro., p. 224)

Lent by Mr. and Mrs. Richard A. Jamison

This pedestal-based card table has lost much of
its painted decoration but has been included
because of its unusual color and relationship to
other pieces of Baltimore painted furniture of
the period. The motif on the front skirt of a
sheathed sword entwined with ribbon is
related to the decoration on the two small
window seats or benches and the sofa in the
Alexander Brown set of painted furniture (cat.
nos. 50 & 51). Painted on the sheath of the sword
are inset panels containing various classical
designs. Applied over the center of this
decoration is a wreath of laurel leaves encircling
an eagle. Oak leaf and acorn wreaths on each
side of the front skirt frame a six-pointed star.
The skirt at each end is decorated with fanlike
anthemion motifs and linear panels much like
those on the Alexander Brown card tables (cat.
no. 52). The edges of the top when closed are
striped and contain a connected scroll and
anthemion design, the classical source for which
could be a similar pattern incised on the inner
cornice of the Athenian Treasury in Delphi
(Lawrence, fig. 83, p. 144). The edges of the
playing surface are also striped, and in each
corner there is a fanlike anthemion motif that
also occurs on the pedestal base.

48   SIDE CHAIR (One of six) ca. 1820-30

Wood painted white with polychrome decoration
Height: 32¼ in.; width: 17½ in.; depth: 16 in.
Provenance: Daingerfield family of *Poplar Hill*,
Prince George's County, Maryland; bequeathed to
the Society by a descendant
Lent by The Maryland Historical Society
Bequest of Mrs. P. B. Key Daingerfield

In its use of turned legs and an elbow form on
the side rails of the seat at the juncture with the
back support, this plank bottom side chair
reveals the Baltimore cabinetmaker's preference
for the antique Roman version of the Greek
klismos chair (see cat. no. 37). The broad crest
rail is edged with green and black and decorated
in sepia with a romantic view of an ancient ruin.
The stay rail as well as both front legs are
decorated with leaf and berry drops in black and
green. These two colors are used again to
decorate the front stretcher, to outline many of
the structural members, and to edge certain of
the turnings of the front legs and back support.
The plank bottom seat has most likely been
repainted in recent years, but it is important to
remember that seats of this kind were covered
with a cushion or a thin layer of upholstery (see
cat. no. 40).

49 SIDE CHAIR (One of twelve) ca. 1820-30

Wood painted yellow and Pompeian red with
polychrome, stenciled and freehand gilt decoration

Height: 31⅝ in.; width: 18⅛ in.; depth: 17⅛ in.

Provenance: Alexander Brown family of Baltimore;
by descent to the present owners

Part of a set of nineteen pieces (see cat. nos. 50-53)

Lent by Mr. and Mrs. Benjamin H. Griswold, III

These twelve painted side chairs are part of a
nineteen piece set of furniture purchased by the
Alexander Brown family sometime between 1820
and 1830. For many years, part of this set has
been in use in the Board Room of Alex.
Brown & Sons, America's oldest investment
banking house, established in Baltimore in 1800.
However, the presence of two card tables, and
certain other non-utilitarian items of furniture
in the set, would indicate that the furniture was
originally intended for domestic use, possibly
for the handsome Greek revival residence,
Mondawmin, purchased by Alexander Brown in
the 1830's. Besides the twelve chairs, there
are in this extraordinary set of Baltimore
painted furniture two card tables, two small
benches or settees, one sofa, a pier table and a
large dining room or banquet table (not
included here).

The basic form of these side chairs is a Roman
version of the Greek klismos chair. Instead of
saber legs, the front legs are straight with
turnings. The painted and stenciled decoration
on the broad, curving crest rail of the back has
a central motif of griffins on each side of an urn,
in turn flanked by gilt Grecian scrolls. Based on
a design by Thomas Sheraton the painting on
these chair backs, though somewhat overpainted,
is closely related to that on the chairs made for
the Abell family of Baltimore (cat. no. 36), and
probably the work of the same ornamenter. In a
panel of Pompeian red on the smaller stay rail
there is Greek key design in black. Rather
heavily-painted, leaf drops appear on each turned
front leg. On each side rail, above the front leg,

there is an anthemion motif often found in other Baltimore painted furniture of this period. On each corner of the front seat rail there is the repeated design of a winged thunderbolt. The striping on the continuous, curvilinear back supports, side rails of the seat, and rear saber legs is extremely similar to that on the Abell family chairs.

The cane seats are removable, perhaps again to facilitate recanning or, according to Baltimore tradition, to be replaced in the winter by heavier, more solid seats.

76

Detail from plate 56, "Ornament for a frieze or Tablet,"
The Cabinet-maker and Upholsterer's Drawing-Book
by Thomas Sheraton
Courtesy of the Henry Francis du Pont Winterthur Museum

50 BENCH OR SETTEE (One of a pair)
ca. 1820-30

Wood painted brown and Pompeian red with
polychrome, stenciled and freehand gilt decoration;
brass mountings

Height: 15¾ in.; length: 45 in.; depth: 16 in.

Provenance: Alexander Brown family of Baltimore;
by descent to the present owners

Part of a set of nineteen pieces (see cat. nos. 49 &
51-53)

Lent by Mr. and Mrs. Benjamin H. Griswold, III

These small, low, cane-seated benches, mounted
on heavy, turned Roman legs, are based on the
antique Roman furniture form called the
biselium — a small couch or settee known to have
been used by the Romans at spectator events.
The predominant decoration occurs on the seat
rail, on which is painted a sheathed sword
entwined with ribbon. The sheath or scabbard is
decorated with panels of classical design (see
cat. no. 51) . At each end above the legs, on a
background of Pompeian red, there is the design
of a winged thunderbolt.

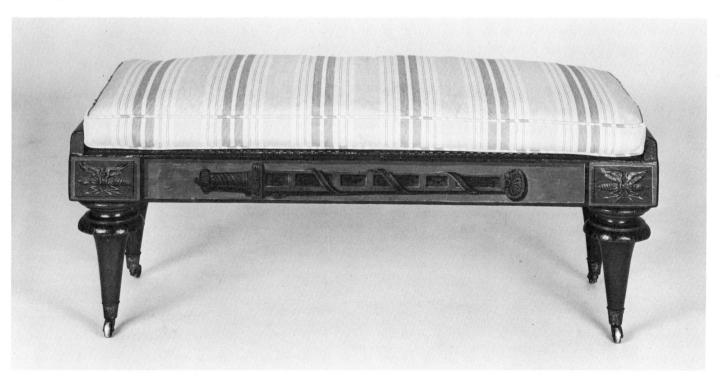

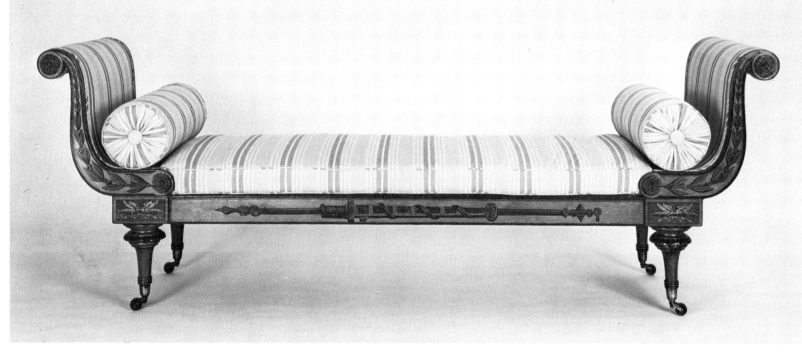

51 SOFA ca. 1820-30

Wood painted yellow and Pompeian red with polychrome, stenciled and freehand gilt decoration; brass mountings

Height: 36 in.; length: 103⅜ in.; depth: 26⅝ in.

Provenance: Alexander Brown family of Baltimore; by descent to the present owners

Part of a set of nineteen pieces (see cat. nos. 49, 50, 52, & 53)

Lent by Mr. and Mrs. Benjamin H. Griswold, III

This Grecian-style sofa, possibly the most important individual piece in the Alexander Brown set of Baltimore painted furniture, has a caned seat and upholstered scroll ends. The gilt and polychrome decoration is on all four sides. The caning was always intended to be covered by a cushion as there are extended structural members on the scroll ends to hold it in place. This sofa is supported by four Roman legs with casters similar to those on the two small benches or settees (cat. no. 50). The same decorative motif of a sheathed sword is repeated but is superimposed over a classical spear or standard. This is one of the few instances when an exact source can be found for a decorative element on Baltimore painted furniture (Percier and Fontaine, pl. 30, 1812 edition). The motif of a winged thunderbolt on a Pompeian-red field is also repeated above each of the four Roman legs. On each side of the scroll ends of the sofa, there are classical laurel and rosette designs in polychromy. Black, gold and brown striping appears as an outline for various structural members of the sofa.

Detail from plate 33, *Recueil de Décorations Intérieures . . .* by C. Percier and P. F. L. Fontaine
Courtesy of George Peabody Branch, Enoch Pratt Free Library

Detail from plate 30, *Recueil de Décorations Intérieures . . .* by C. Percier and P. F. L. Fontaine
Courtesy of George Peabody Branch, Enoch Pratt Free Library

52 CARD TABLE (One of a pair) ca. 1820-30

Mahogany, wood painted yellow and Pompeian red with polychrome, stenciled and freehand gilt decoration; brass mountings

Height: 28⅜ in.; width: 36⅛ in.; depth: 17⅞ in.

Provenance: Alexander Brown family of Baltimore; by descent to the present owners

Part of a set of nineteen pieces (see cat. nos. 49-51 & 53)

Lent by Mr. and Mrs. Benjamin H. Griswold, III

Of the various pieces of painted furniture made for the Alexander Brown family, this pair of card tables with mahogany tops retains more of its original decoration than any other piece. The painted panels on all sides of the skirt are especially well preserved. On the long skirts, the stenciled and freehand gilt decoration, derived from designs by Thomas Sheraton, is imposed on a Pompeian-red background. This same motif is found on the chairs in this set (cat. no. 49) and is related to that on the chair backs of another set of painted, Baltimore klismos chairs (cat. no. 36). On the card tables, this design is flanked at each end by the repeated design motif of a winged thunderbolt in black and two shades of green. The skirt at each end is decorated with fanlike palmettes flanking linear, rectangular panels. The tables are supported by a turned, pedestal base set on an X-frame, mounted on Roman feet with casters. Acanthus leaf decoration appears on the hub of the base, and the palmette design is repeated on the front and back of this turned, hub base. On the sides of each member of the X-frame, again in two tones of green paint, there is a scroll design terminating in a grotesque eaglelike head.

The two leaves, when open, swivel to form the playing surface. There is an interior storage compartment lined with mulberry-colored velvet.

53 PIER TABLE ca. 1820-30

Wood painted yellow and Pompeian red with polychrome, stenciled and freehand gilt decoration; mirror back and brass mountings

Height: 34¼ in.; width: 38 in.; depth: 18⅝ in.

Provenance: Alexander Brown family of Baltimore; by descent to the present owners

Part of a set of nineteen pieces (see cat. nos. 49-52)

Lent by Mr. and Mrs. Benjamin H. Griswold, III

The predominant decoration of this columnar, mirror-backed pier table repeats that found on the card table (cat. no. 52) and side chairs (cat. no. 49) in the Alexander Brown set of Baltimore painted furniture. On the skirt of this pier table, there is the repeated motif of an urn flanked by griffins and acanthus leaf Greek scrolls — all based on a design by Sheraton. The same leaf scroll design with rosettes appears on the side framing of the mirror back. The decoration of a winged thunderbolt in two shades of green and black, found on the skirt of each card table, is repeated here at the top of each of the front supports and a palmette or anthemion decoration is on the end skirts. Multiple colors are used in the striping of the turned, columnar, front supports and the center ring turnings are decorated with gilt. The bulbous form at the base of each column may be of Egyptian origin and is decorated with polychrome acanthus leaves. The top and base are painted to imitate Sienna marble.

54   ARMCHAIR (One of a pair) ca. 1830-40

Wood grained to simulate rosewood with stenciled and freehand gilt decoration

Height: 34¼ in.; width: 20⅞ in.; depth: 17¾ in.

Part of a set of twelve chairs; four side chairs, Baltimore Museum; six side chairs, private collection

The Baltimore Museum of Art
Gift of Mrs. Henry V. Ward   34.56.1 & 2

These armchairs, in their modified klismos form, still retain some of the earlier features of the classical, archaeological style. This is especially evident in the saber-shaped, front and rear legs and the curvilinear side rails and back supports. The scroll arms rest on gilt balls which are joined to the seat rails. Gilt acanthus leaves, Grecian scrolls, stylized anthemia, as well as gold striping, are used as decoration on the chair back, and certain of these elements occur again on the front seat rail. Acanthus leaf decoration appears at the top of each of the front legs, and their connecting stretcher is ornamented with laurel.

55 PIER TABLE ca. 1830-40

Wood painted black with gilt decoration
Height: 34¼ in.; width: 42⅛ in.; depth: 22⅜ in.
Lent by James M. Goode

This pier table is supported by a heavy,
columnar, pedestal base, with scroll legs. Gilt
decoration appears on all four sides of the skirt,
on the turned columnar support, and on all sides
of the four scroll legs. In the center of the two
long sides of the decorated skirt there appear the
initials *O'B*, framed by a wreath of acorns and
leaves. This is flanked at each side by Greek
scrolls and anthemion designs at the center of
which are small vases or compotes containing
fruit. These latter designs are repeated on the
skirt ends. A different acorn and leaf design in
gilt appears at the top of the columnar support.
Gold acanthus leaves outline the edges of each
scroll leg at the termination of which are
painted gilt rosettes. On two of the four sides of
the base of the columnar support there is a much
repeated, decorative device in Baltimore painted
furniture of a winged thunderbolt.

It is thought that the initials *O'B* stand for a
Baltimore family named O'Brien. The name
O'Brien, with various surnames, does appear in
the Baltimore City Directories in the first four
decades of the 19th century.

The table was purchased at auction and
purportedly had a Baltimore provenance.

56   PIER TABLE ca. 1830-40

Wood grained to simulate rosewood with polychrome,
stenciled and freehand decoration and freehand
bronzing; slate top, mirror back and brass mountings

Height: 39¾ in.; width: 44½ in.; depth: 21½

Lent by Peter Hill

The slate top of this pier table is marbelized in
the same manner as its base. On three sides of the
skirt or apron of the table top, there is a polychrome, stenciled design of fruit and foliage with
the addition of freehand bronzing. Such stenciled
designs were often employed by the ornamenters
of Baltimore painted furniture (see cat. nos. 30
& 34). The wooden framing of the mirror back
is grained to simulate rosewood. Applied over
this graining at each side of the mirror, there is
a double-ended standard with acanthus leaves
and a fanlike anthemion at each termination.
The two turned and reeded front supports are
based on a classic Roman design source.
Turnings at the top of these supports, the
center section and the animal paw feet are
gilded. Other areas of these legs or supports are
grained to simulate rosewood. The structural
platform base is related to another Baltimore
pier table in the classical, archaeological style
(see cat. no. 35).

57 MUSIC STOOL ca. 1830-40

Wood painted black with gilt decoration; cast iron
and brass mountings

Height: 34½ in.; diameter of the seat: 14½ in.

Provenance: Lowndes family of Annapolis

Lent by the Colonial Dames of America, Chapter I
Gift of Mrs. W. Bladen Lowndes

This music or piano stool has a swivel seat
mounted on a tripod base with animal feet — the
whole richly carved with acanthus leaves. Gilt
decoration appears on a turning in the center of
the pedestal base. The center of the three
moldings at the base of the upholstered seat is
also enriched with gilt decoration. The back
support in the form of a winged lyre and
curvilinear side or arm supports are cast iron
with bronze gilding. The wooden crest rail is
painted and ornamented with the repeated form
of a lyre flanked by Grecian scrolls. The wooden
support for the metal back is decorated with gilt
anthemia and palmettes and applied brass
rosettes.

85

58   PIANOFORTE ca. 1830-40

Mahogany with maple and mahogany veneer and
satinwood inlay; stenciled and freehand gilt
decoration; brass mountings

Height: 36 in.; width: 67 in.; depth: 32½

Pianoforte maker: Joseph Hisky (born Vienna,
died Baltimore, 1848)

Lent by Peter Hill

The rectangular case of this pianoforte is supported by two lyre form, pedestal bases with
brass animal paw feet and casters. The lyre forms
are decorated in gilt motifs of laurel leaves and
berries, and an acorn and oak leaf design occurs
on the connecting scroll stretcher. Gilt decoration also appears on the pedal support in the
form of stylized organ pipes. The front of the
fall-board is ebonized and enriched with applied
gilt scroll decoration of classical origin.

The pastoral scene above the keyboard and the
legend of Joseph Hisky is actually an engraving
which presumably was hand-colored and edged
with gilt after its application. The engraving is
by Medairy and Bannerman after a drawing
by S. Smith. The names William Bannerman and
John Medairy do not appear as a partnership in
the Baltimore City Directories until 1831. The
listing continues in the next City Directory of
1833 but is not present in 1835. The name S.
Smith probably refers to Samuel Smith, "artist
and drawing master in Baltimore" (Groce and
Wallace, p. 590) . Joseph Hisky, pianoforte
maker, is first listed in the City Directory in 1819.

59 PIANOFORTE ca. 1830-40

Mahogany with mahogany veneer and satinwood inlay; stenciled and freehand gilt decoration; brass mountings

Height: 36¼ in.; width: 67⅛ in.; depth: 32 in.

Pianoforte maker: Joseph Hisky (born Vienna, died Baltimore, 1848)

The Baltimore Museum of Art
Anonymous Gift 42.36

The shape of the rectangular case of this piano is nearly identical to the other Hisky piano included here (cat. no. 58), and the same hand-colored engraving appears above the keyboard. However, there is variation in the decorative design in the freehand and stenciled gilt decoration as well as in the use of a columnar pedestal base rather than the lyre form. In the top, or case section of the piano, gilt decoration is only found in a leaf, ribbon and flower cartouche that forms an ornamental escutcheon on the ebonized band that encircles the base of the case. The base of the pedal support is of gilt with gesso moldings. Applied in gilt on the face of this suspended pedal support are gilt acanthus leaves with scroll ends supporting a basket of fruit. On the outer sides of both pedestal supports is a gilt anthemion. Gilt laurel sprays are found on the top of each leg. The turnings of the columnar supports are further enriched by the application of gilt.

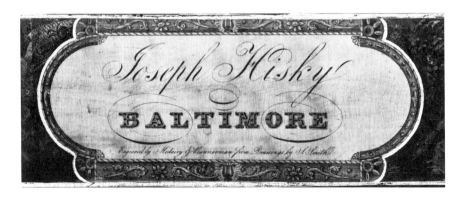

NOTES ON TREATMENT OF PAINTED FURNITURE

SOFA (cat. no. 51) after filling of paint losses, prior to inpainting

Of all the furniture brought into the Baltimore Museum, the set made for the Alexander Brown family (cat. nos. 49-53) required the most extensive treatment. With the exception of the side chairs, all pieces were restored in varying degrees depending upon the security of the paint and its appearance.

The construction of painted furniture is similar to that of an easel painting — a basic wood support covered with layers of ground, painted designs and a resinous surface coating. On the pieces in the Alexander Brown set, the ground layers consisted of a light ochre paint with a transparent dark tone painted over it. The freehand and stenciled design layer was composed of gold, Pompeian-red and other polychromy which was applied by a brush. The top layer was a transparent, natural resin coating.

The wood moves, shrinks and swells according to the moisture content of the air around it. However, the paint layers, hardened with age, are not flexible, and therefore break free when the wood underneath them moves. The results of this process, plus deterioration due to constant use, could be seen on many pieces in this set of painted furniture when they came to the Baltimore Museum.

There were many ground and paint losses and also many areas where these layers were starting to flake. The first part of the treatment was to secure the flaking. In order to hold the loosened pieces of ground and paint in their correct place, pieces of strong, porous Japanese paper were laid over them while hot gelatine size was brushed on, thin enough to flow under the loose flakes. The moisture in the size was absorbed with newsprint paper while the treated flaking was pressed down and the areas further dried and consolidated with a warm tacking iron. The papers were removed with a damp cotton swab.

The colors of the paint on the furniture were obscured by the accumulation of grime. This was removed with a wax-emulsion cleaner, and the residue of the cleaner was wiped away with a mild petroleum solvent. The resinous coating was not removed because it had not darkened to the extent of obscuring the colors under it. Due to the depth of the ground and paint losses, some areas had to be filled in order to bring them to the same level as the surrounding paint. The material used was a water soluble, synthetic, claylike filler bonded with polyvinyl acetate emulsion.

To separate the inpainting from the original paint and to facilitate the color matching for the inpainting process, a coating of a synthetic varnish was brushed over all the painted areas including the fillings. The inpainting was done with leached oil paints mixed into a synthetic resin. The most extensive losses were on the benches or settees. The design of the sword and scabbard on one of the long sides of one bench had almost been entirely lost. To replace the design a stencil was made by photographing the design on the companion piece and enlarging it to the exact measurements. The photograph was transferred with carbon paper to the side of the bench and then repainted.

The final step in the treatment process was an application of a synthetic varnish by brush and then by airbrush which reduced the gloss and gave the pieces a uniform semi-matte finish.

A card table (cat. no. 14) with an architectural view of *Mount Clare* did not have extensive paint losses, but the colors in some of the designs were completely obscured by thick coatings of a hard resin, possibly copal varnish, which had turned brown with age. It was found that these could be removed by the careful application of solvents. After the cleaning of the architectural view of *Mount Clare,* the decision was made to remove the coatings from the rest of the designs to make the table more uniform in appearance.

After cleaning, a synthetic non-yellowing varnish was brushed on and the most noticeable losses were inpainted with leached oils in a plastic medium. To complete the procedure the entire table was sprayed with a synthetic varnish.

During the cleaning process, we found the general construction of the paint layers as follows. The table was completely covered with black paint, even under the painting of *Mount Clare.* The scrolls and background decoration on the legs and skirt are a copper-colored gilt which was applied on top of the black as was the yellow striping on the legs. The white paint making up the designs on the legs and side panels of the table are painted directly on the gilt. Since the roofline of the building at the extreme left of the architectural view extends over the gilt lines framing the painting, it is apparent that the scroll decoration was applied before. The final step was to apply a thin black border on the two sides and bottom of the architectural scene.

Victor C. B. Covey
Senior Conservator

Kay Silberfeld
Conservator

91

CARD TABLE (cat. no. 14) with partial varnish removal

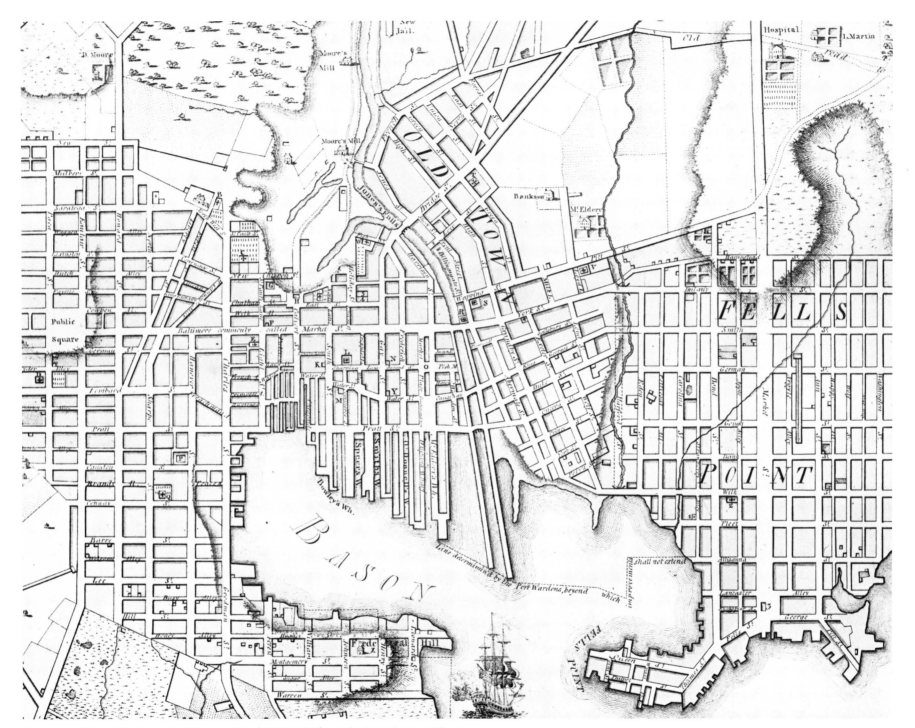

Plan of the City and Environs of Baltimore, 1801 Courtesy of The Peabody Institute, Baltimore

CABINETMAKERS AND ALLIED TRADESMEN WORKING IN BALTIMORE 1800-1840

This list of Baltimore cabinetmakers and chairmakers who were working between 1800 and 1840 has been compiled from the Baltimore City Directories which, for those years, were published in 1800-01, 1802, 1803, 1804, 1807, 1808, 1810, 1812, 1814-15, 1816, 1817-18, 1819, 1822-23, 1824, 1827, 1829, 1831, 1833, 1835, 1837 and 1840. We have marked with an asterisk those individuals listed as fancy or ornamental chairmakers, ornamental painters, fancy chair painters and other craftsmen who have special relevance to the furniture included here.

During this forty year period, as well as in the latter years of the 18th century and until the great Baltimore fire of 1904 (which destroyed 140 acres of downtown Baltimore), the cabinetmaking industry was located in three separate areas of the city, referred to as Baltimore, Old Town and Fells Point.

Although there had been settlements near the basin west of the confluence of Jones Falls and the Patapsco in the mid-17th century, the town called Baltimore was not laid out until 1730 when 60 acres were divided into a grid plan. Just east of Jones Falls was an even older settlement, Jonestown which was incorporated in 1732, through an act of the Maryland Assembly, and always known as Old Town. Thirteen years later, in 1745, an act of the Assembly united these two towns which henceforth were to be under the name of Baltimore. There was still another independent settlement in the area. In 1730, a William Fell, ship carpenter, had purchased a tract of land called Copus Harbor, located at what is now called Fells Point, at the foot of Broadway. Here Mr. Fell divided his land into city lots. The water was deep at the point and it soon became a ship building as well as a trading center, and for many years the two settlements, Baltimore and Fells Point, were openly competing with one another. Finally in 1773, as the two towns developed toward each other and practically connected, Fells Point became a part of Baltimore.

Although united under the name of Baltimore, each area retained its own identity. The directories themselves illustrate this fact in refining an address by indicating that it is in Fells Point or Old Town. Where there is no indication, the location is assumed to be the section of the city west of the Falls.

In the forty year period covered here, the cultural, social and business center of the city was in the area west of Jones Falls. In 1815, the gifted French architect, Maximilien Godefroy, had designed the Battle Monument and soon Monument Square became the most fashionable residential area of the city. There were in addition great houses on South and Water Streets, near the Baltimore Exchange. The Baltimore cabinetmakers, Hugh and John Finlay, Robert Fisher and Thomas S. Renshaw, all had shops on Gay Street. Baltimore street, earlier called Market Street, was the great east-west thoroughfare of the city. This was the first street in the city to be paved and here was located most of the city's trade and business. Besides cabinetmakers, there were portrait and miniature painters, sellers and hangers of wallpapers, upholsterers, and shops offering all types of merchandise. There are also, of course, cabinet-makers and related craftsmen listed as working or living in other parts of the city, usually in the still well defined business and tradesmen's areas of Fells Point and Old Town.

In the Preface to the 1833 Directory, the publisher, Richard J. Matchett, commented:

"from the commencement of taking the citizens' names, to binding the book he has met difficulty . . . at every step. . . . He has, however, completed his task, and if he has not done (the best his circumstances allows in it) , he will say, he hopes never to be engaged in a more dis-agreeable one. The task of visiting every house in the city. . . ., of spelling names (for which there is no rule) pronounced alike but spelt differently, of meeting rebuffs from the ignorant and impudent. . . . , the erroneous charge . . . of our having omitted names, by those who have not information sufficient to know where to examine for them, of mis-spelling of not putting a more full direction, etc. etc." was certainly not easy.

Mr. Matchett's problems are the same we found in compiling our list, and we must admit that it perpetuates the errors found in the Directories. The most common ones are mis-spellings of names and addresses, omission of a name which might appear in the preceding and following years, and confusing addresses. It is not always clear that a man's business address, as opposed to his home address, is given. Quite often, the first floor of a house was a shop or office with the living quarters one or two stories above, which meant that businesses and residences were commonly mingled on the same block.

The following compilation is a list of names rather than of individuals. For instance, two men with the same name have been grouped together under one heading although the listings are separated by several years. We have chosen the most common or logical spelling, or where this was not apparent, we have given alternate spellings. Following the names is the man's occupation as he listed himself in the

Directory; if this listing changed year by year, we have indicated it by giving all the listings. Where a business address and a home address are both known, we have listed them separately. The dates in parentheses indicate the issue of the Directory from which the information preceding them has come. Finally, we have repeated the following abbreviations: f.p. for Fells Point, o.t. for Old Town, and f.h. for Federal Hill (addresses in Federal Hill occur only in a few instances). Where no initials occur, the location is understood to be west of Jones Falls near the basin.

John and Hugh Finley

HAVE opened a shop at No. 190½, Market-street, opposite Mr Peter Wyant's inn, where they have for sale, and make to any pattern, all kinds of FANCY and JAPANNED FURNITURE, viz.

Japanned and gilt card, pier, tea, dressing, writing and shaving TABLES, with or without views adjacent to the city.

Ditto cane seats, rush and windsor CHAIRS, with or without views.

Ditto cane seats, rush and windsor SETTEES, with or without views.

Ditto Window and Recess Seats.

Ditto Wash and Candle Stands.

Ditto Fire and Candle Screens.

Ditto   Ditto.   with views.

Ditto Bedsteads, and Bed and Window Cornices, &c.

Which they warrant equal to any imported.

They as usual execute Coach, Sign and Ornamental Painting.

Military standards, drums, masonic aprons, all kinds of silk transparencies, &c. in the neatest manner, and on the shortest notice.

☞ Old chairs repainted.

N. B. Apply as above or at their manufactory No. 3, South Frederick-street.

October 24.   d

Federal Gazette and Baltimore Daily Advertiser, 24 October 1803

WILLIAM ABEY, cabinetmaker, Cross Street west of Johnson (1831) ; William Street near Cross (1835, 1840)

JOHN AIRMOND, chairmaker, Lombard Street (1800-01)

JOHN ALBRIGHT, piano forte maker, Liberty Street (1800-01)

JOHN ALEXANDER, cabinetmaker, Barry Street, shop, corner of Hanover and Baltimore Streets (1800-01) ; No. 19 Market Space (1802) ; Lexington Street (1803)

ISAAC ALLEN, cabinetmaker, Little York, south side west of Exeter (1822-23)

WILLIAM ALLEN, portable writing desk manufacturer, 5 N. Liberty Street, dwelling, Fayette near Eutaw Street (1829)

SAMUEL ANDERSON, cabinet and chairmaker, dwelling and shop, East Street (1800-01)

GEORGE ARMSTRONG, chairmaker, northeast corner of High and Water Streets (1833)

THOMAS ARMSTRONG, cabinetmaker, near Gay in East Street (1802)

*WILLIAM ARMSTRONG, fancy chairmaker, 97 Bond Street, dwelling, 103 Bond Street, f.p. (1829) ; chairmaker, corner of Strawberry Alley and E. Baltimore Street (1837)

GEORGE ARNOLD, chairmaker, Carpenter's Alley north side east of Paca (1829)

*NICHOLAS J. ASH, fancy painter, Eden north of Baltimore Street (1837)

JAMES ASKEY, cabinetmaker, Stiles Street near S. Exeter (1833) ; Charles Street east of Montgomery (1840)

JOHN ATWOOD, cabinetmaker, northeast corner of Hanover and Lombard Streets (1829) ; 39 Water Street (1831, 1833) ; corner of North Street and Orange Alley, dwelling, Calvert Street near Baltimore (1835) ; corner of North Street and Orange Alley, dwelling, Calvert Street near Mulberry (1837) ; corner of North Street and Orange Alley, dwelling, Monument Street east of Constitution (1840)

LEWIS AUODOUN, cabinetmaker, Wilk Street near Argyle Alley (1833)

COLEGATE AUSTEN, cabinetmaker, Fayette Street east of Pine (1827)

GEORGE AUSTEN, firm of Hiss and Austen, cabinet and chair factory, 23 Fayette Street, dwelling, Howard Street east side south of Brandy Alley (1822-23) ; factory, 23 Fayette Street, dwelling, 21 Fayette Street (1827, 1829, 1831) ; factory, 23 Fayette Street, dwelling, 77 W. Fayette Street (1833, 1835)

SMITH BACHELOR/BACHLOR, cabinetmaker, 23 Carolina Street, f.p. (1819) ; William's Alley, south side east of Spring (1822-23)

JOHN BACKMAN, cabinetmaker, 57 S. Charles Street (1824)

WASHINGTON BAIN/BAYNE, cabinetmaker, Bridge Street west side north of French (1822-23) ; Potter Street west side north of Gay (1827)

BART BAKER, chairmaker, Aliceanna Street north of Argyle Alley, f.p. (1819)

HILARY C. BAKER, cabinetmaker, Eden Street south of Mullikin (1835) ; N. Gay Street near Mott (1837) ; corner of Howard and Wayne Streets (1840)

ROBERT BAKER, cabinetmaker, Vine Alley west of Pine street (1833) ; Pearl Street west of Fayette (1835) ; Park Lane east of Pine Street (1840)

WILLIAM BAKER, chairmaker, corner of Potter and Douglass Streets (1837)

ISAIAH BALDERSTON, cabinetmaker, Whiskey Alley (1817-18)

LEVI BANJAMIN, dealer in furniture, 12 Caroline Row, Caroline Street (1833)

THOMAS BARLOW, cabinetmaker, Caroline Street north of Baltimore (1837)

*WILLIAM BARNES, coachmaker, 62 Cumberland Row (1808) ; sign and ornamental painter, 8 Bridge Street, o.t. (1816)

*JOHN BARNHART, letterer and sign painter, York Avenue (1822-23, 1824) ; letterer, York Avenue, o.t. (1827) ; ornamental painter, York Avenue, o.t. (1829)

JOHN M. BARRETT, cabinetmaker, dwelling, 52 Harrison Street (1812, 1814-15)

BARRETT & RINGGOLD, cabinetmakers, 5 Great York Street, o.t. (1812)

THOMAS BARRETT, ebonist, Harrison Street (1800-01)

D. B. BARRON, cabinetmaker, Hill street west of Hanover (1835)

JAMES B. BARRON, cabinetmaker, Cider Alley (1817-18) ; rear of 46 W. Pratt Street (1827) ; Busy Alley between Charles and Hanover Streets (1829, 1831)

JOHN B. BARRY, his cabinet wareroom, 3 Light Street (1804)

JOSEPH BARRY, cabinet and upholstery wareroom, next door to the Fountain Inn, and at 130 S. Second Street, Philadelphia (1803)

WASHINGTON BARRY, cabinetmaker, Bridge Street, north side east of French, o.t. (1824)

JULIUS BARTHOLOMEE, cabinetmaker, 103 N. Howard Street (1812)

WILLIAM BARTLETT, piano forte maker, 20 Fayette Street (1822-23, 1824, 1827)

*GASSAWAY BASSFORD, fancy and windsor chair-maker, 68 S. Charles Street (1829, 1831) ; ornamental painter, 13 Thomson Street (1835) ; chairmaker, 13 Thompson Street (1837)

BASSFORD & McDONALD, chair factory, 68 S. Charles Street (1833)

*CORNELIUS BATES, ornamental painter, Holliday Street (1817-18)

JOHN BAUGHMAN, cabinetmaker, 57 S. Charles Street (1837)

GREENBURY BAXTER, cabinetmaker, southeast corner of Bridge and Front Streets, dwelling, Green Street east side of Low (1822-23)

ROBERT BEAKER, cabinetmaker, Park Lane east of Pine Street (1837)

HENRY BEATSON, cabinetmaker, 105 Lombard Street west of Howard (1835, 1837, 1840)

SEBASTIAN BEHLAR, cabinetmaker, Pinkney Street near Caroline (1833)

GEORGE BENNETT, cabinetmaker, southwest corner of Bridge and East Streets, o.t. (1824) ; Low Street, north side, 1 door west of Potter, o.t. (1829) ; Baltimore Street west of Cove (1833)

JOHN BAPTIST BERSON, cabinetmaker, 54 Harrison Street (1810)

JOHN BETTS, cabinetmaker, Bond Street 1 door south of Aliceanna (1840)

REUBEN A. L. BEVANS, cabinetmaker, Caroline Row, Caroline Street (1835, 1837) ; Baltimore Street east of Caroline (1840)

SAMUEL BEVAN, cabinetmaker, 33 W. Pratt Street (1829)

JAMES BILLINGTON, cabinetmaker, Milk Lane, o.t. (1816, 1817-18, 1819) ; Smith Street, north side east of Spring (1822-23) ; Harford Run, east side south of Baltimore (1824, 1827) ; East Street north of Pitt, o.t. (1829, 1831, 1833)

DAVID BISHOP, cabinetmaker, 16 New Church Street (1833) ; East Street south of French (1835) ; Forrest Street west of Harford Run (1837, 1840)

BENJAMIN BLACKISTON, chairmaker, E. Pratt Street near the bridge (1817-18)

BLACKISTON & ELDER, cabinetmakers, Cove Street, 1 door south of Sarah Ann (1840)

JOHN B. BLACKISTON, cabinetmaker, Saratoga Street near Liberty (1833) ; Cove Street south of Mulberry (1835, 1837, 1840)

BLACKSTON & BEARY, cabinetmakers, 27 S. Calvert Street (1833)

LEONARD BLADES, chairmaker, 31 Exeter Street (1835)

WILLIAM H. BLASS, cabinetmaker, Comet Street (1835) ; Greene Street north of Burgundy Alley (1837) ; 58 Sterling Street (1840)

ABEL BOARDMAN, furniture wareroom, Water Street north of Commerce (1817-18)

DAVID BODENSICK/BODDENSTICK, cabinetmaker, Fayette Street near Pine (1833) ; Mulberry Street west of Pearl (1835) ; Mulberry Street east of Pine (1837, 1840)

FREDERICK BOLKERN, cabinetmaker, corner of Exeter and Wilk Streets (1840)

CHARLES BOOBELT, cabinetmaker, Eutaw Street south of Monument (1837)

JOHN H. D. BOON, chairmaker, Holland Street near Aisquith, o.t. (1829) ; N. Gay Street near Belle Air Market (1831)

WILLIAM BOON, cabinetmaker, Cowpen Alley west of Liberty Street (1840)

JAMES BOOZ, chairmaker, Aliceanna Street east of Wolf (1840)

JOHN B. BOSSIER, cabinetmaker, Granby Street near Gough (1833)

BARTHOLOMEW BOSTON, piano forte maker, 35 Saratoga Street (1814-15, 1816) ; Mulberry Street near North (1817-18) ; 36 Saratoga Street (1819)

*DAVID P. BOULDEN, ornamental painter, Hillen Street east of Front (1837, 1840)

ISAAC BOWERS, cabinetmaker, 25 N. Exeter Street (1837) ; 23 N. Exeter Street (1840)

JOSEPH K. BOYD. upholsterer and cabinetmaker, southeast corner of South and Water Streets (1831)

BRADFORD & RINGGOLD, cabinetmakers, 23 Fayette Street (1817-18)

WILLIAM BRADSHIRE, cabinetmaker, 108 Green Street, o.t. (1803)

FERDINAND BRANDES, cabinetmaker, corner of York Street and X (sic) Alley (1840)

FREDERICK BRANDES, cabinetmaker, corner of Grant and Lombard Streets (1837)

JOHN BRADLEY BRASHEARS, cabinetmaker, Granby Street east of Gough (1831) ; Lunn's Lane north of Conway Street (1835) ; separately listed at Argyle Alley and Lancaster Streets (1835) ; 125 S. Sharp Street (1837) ; 59 Albemarle Street (1840)

BRASHEARS & RENWICK, cabinetmakers, 84½ Howard Street north of Saratoga (1840)

THOMAS BRASHEARS, chairmaker, 53 S. Howard Street (1837)

JOHN BRENAN, cabinetmaker, 10 Frederick Street near Baltimore (1837)

DANIEL BREWER, furniture wareroom, 33 Harrison Street (1831) ; cabinetmaker, 27 Harrison Street (1833, 1835, 1837) ; 68 N. Howard Street (1840)

RICHARD BRIGGS, cabinetmaker, Fleet Street west of Happy Alley (1835) ; Chestnut Alley east of Pearl Street (1837) ; Apple Alley south of Baltimore Street (1840)

JOHN BRIGHTMAN/BRIGHTMORE, cabinetmaker, corner of Eutaw Street and Dutch Alley (1827, 1829) ; Mulberry Street west of Eutaw (1837)

HARMAN H. BRINNING, cabinetmaker, Barre Street west of Sharp (1840)

CHARLES BRIZARD, cabinetmaker, 54 S. Charles Street (1814-15) ; 33 S. Charles Street (1816, 1817-18, 1819) ; 44 Marsh Market Space (1822-23)

HAMMOND BROCHMAN, cabinetmaker, Commerce Street between Pratt and Cable (1835)

WILLIAM BROOKS, cabinetmaker, 63 N. Front Street (1837)

JAMES BROOM, cabinetmaker, Wolf Street north of Thames (1835)

GEORGE BROWN, cabinetmaker, 107 Green Street (1837)

a

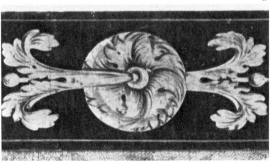

JACOB BROWN, cabinetmaker, Aisquith Street near McElderry, o.t. (1829)

JOSEPH BROWN, cabinetmaker, back of 109 High Street, o.t. (1803); 113 High Street (1804); South Street (1807); also listed at 31 N. Gay Street (1807, 1808)

WILLIAM BROWN, cabinetmaker, 109 High Street, o.t. (1800-01, 1803)

HERMAN BRUNING, cabinetmaker, 7 Sharp Street (1835); Baltimore Street east of Cove (1837)

WILLIAM BRUSHWILLER/BRUSHWELL, cabinetmaker, Briton Street north of Monument (1835); chairmaker, Sterling Street near Madison (1837); Abraham Street near Harford Avenue (1840)

JOSHUA BULL, cabinetmaker, Water Street (1803)

PATRICK BURKE, cabinetmaker, 102 Bond Street (1804); cabinet and chairmaker, 61 W. Wilk Street, f.p. (1807, 1808); cabinetmaker, Thames Street, south side east of Market (1827)

JEFFERSON BURN, cabinetmaker, Tripolet's Alley near Baltimore Street (1833, 1837); Ross Street west of Eutaw (1840)

WILLIAM BURTON, cabinetmaker, Eutaw Street south of Lexington, dwelling, Dutch Alley west of Howard Street (1831, 1833); northeast corner of Exeter and Marion Streets (1835)

ANDREW BUSH, cabinetmaker, Ensor Street north of Monument (1837)

CATHERINE BUSH, furniture room, 14 Harrison Street (1840)

JAMES BUSH, furniture store, 17 Harrison Street (1819); furniture warehouse, 14 & 17 Harrison Street (1829, 1831, 1833)

JAMES BYRNE, cabinetmaker, northeast corner of Frederick and Second Streets (1831, 1833, 1835, 1837, 1840)

PETER BYRNE, cabinetmaker, Ross Street east of Paca (1835, 1837, 1840)

THOMAS BYRNE, cabinetmaker, 21 Mulberry Street west of Park (1840)

JAMES A. CALDWELL, chair factory, 27 S. Calvert Street (1840)

JOSEPH CALDWELL, cabinetmaker, 11 South Street, dwelling, adjoining Mrs. Wintkle's tavern, Holliday Street (1816); corner of Water and Frederick Streets (1817-18); 49 Water Street (1819)

WILLIAM CALHOUN, chairmaker, near 30 W. Aliceanna Street (1804)

ISAAC CAMP, cabinet furniture warehouse, Concord Street, east side south of Water (1824, 1827); cabinetmaker, Concord Street north of Pratt (1829); Baltimore Street east of Cove (1833); piano forte maker, Baltimore Street west of Pine (1835)

JOHN CAMP, cabinetmaker, southwest corner of Water and Grant Streets (1831)

WILLIAM CAMP, cabinetmaker, dwelling, 26 Water Street (1802, 1803, 1804, 1807, 1808, 1810, 1814-15, 1816, 1817-18, 1819, 1822-23); manufactory, Jones Falls between Water and Pratt Streets (1817-18); warehouse, Concord Street, east side north of Pratt (1822-23)

JAMES CAMPBELL, cabinetmaker, Franklin Row (1833)

JOHN CAREY, cabinetmaker, Jefferson Street, south side east of Short (1822-23, 1824, 1827, 1829, 1831, 1833, 1835, 1837)

JNO. CAREY, chairmaker, Caroline Street south of Wilk (1837)

*SAMUEL CARIS, gilder, 79 Harrison Street (1833)

JESSE CARTER, chairmaker, 63 N. Liberty Street (1824); Lombard Street west of Eutaw (1829)

JOHN CARTER, chairmaker, Washington Street south side west of Green (1824)

PETER CARTER, chair bottomer, corner of Sharp and Hill Streets (1833)

JAMES CAVE, cabinetmaker, 66 Harrison Street (1817-18)

CAVE & MUNROE, cabinetmakers, 31 Harrison Street (1816)

JAMES CHALMERS, cabinetmaker, Liberty Street near Saratoga (1840)

MARTIN CHANCEAULME, cabinetmaker, Orleans Street west of Aisquith (1835, 1837, 1840)

THOMAS CHANDLER, chairmaker, Aisquith Street, o.t. (1817-18) ; Pitt Street, north side east of Eden (1822-23)

*J. CHAPPEL, sign and ornamental painter, 208 Baltimore Street (1812)

THOMAS CHARTRESS, cabinetmaker, 50 Jones Street, o.t. (1824) ; 50 N. Front Street (1827, 1829, 1831, 1833) ; Holliday Street near Bath (1837)

*WILLIAM CHESTNUT, fancy chairmaker, Hillen Street between High and Front (1829) ; ornamental chairmaker, Hillen Street (1831)

*ABRAHAM CHEVALIER, carver and gilder, Roger's Alley near N. Calvert Street (1800-01)

ABSALOM CHRISFIELD, chair manufactory, 5 S. Calvert Street (1807, 1808)

CHRISFIELD & EGAN, cabinetmakers, 89 W. Pratt Street (1831)

LEVIN CLARIDGE, cabinetmaker, 71 Apple Alley, f.p. (1817-18) ; corner of Ann and Fleet Streets, f.p. (1819)

LEVIN P. CLARK, cabinetmaker, southeast corner of Low and Green Streets, o.t. (1824) ; 14 N. Exeter Street (1831) ; 16 N. Exeter Street (1833)

LEONARD CLARK, cabinetmaker, Potter Street, west side south of Low (1827)

SAMUEL CLARK, chairmaker, 46 Front Street, o.t. (1807, 1808)

*CLARK & WALLIS, fancy chairmakers, 17 S. Gay Street (1812)

*SEPTIMUS CLAYPOOLE, fancy chairmaker, 8 N. Gay Street (1833) ; chairmaker, Hillen Street west of High (1835) ; chair manufactory, Water Street near Gay, dwelling, Hillen Street west of Exeter (1837) ; chair manufacturer, 128 N. High Street (1840)

JAMES P. CLEMONS, cabinetmaker, Fayette Street east of Hanover (1831)

J. B. CLEMMONS, cabinetmaker, Paca Street 1 door from Fayette (1833)

WILLIAM CLEMMONS, cabinetmaker, 6 Harrison Street (1827) ; Pennsylvania Avenue south of Biddle Street (1829, 1831, 1833, 1835, 1840)

JACOB CLINE, cabinetmaker, Charles Street east of Montgomery (1840)

RICHARD COCHRAN, cabinetmaker, Lemmon Street (1837)

COCHRANE & BROTHER, cabinetmakers, 29 Hanover Street north of Lombard, dwelling, 142 Sharp Street 3 doors south of Lee (1840)

COHEN & EYTINGE, furniture store, 41 N. Howard Street (1840)

FREDERICK COLE, chairmaker, 8 High Street, o.t. (1816) ; turner, 6 High Street, o.t. (1817-18) ; chairmaker and turner, Bridge Street north of Union, o.t. (1819)

GEORGE COLE, chairmaker and joiner, 1 High Street (1804) ; chair and spinning wheel maker, 8 High Street, o.t. (1810) ; chairmaker, 6 High Street, o.t. (1814-15, 1816, 1817-18)

GODFRED COLE, chairmaker, 8 High Street, o.t. (1800-01) ; windsor chairmaker, 8 High Street (1802) ; 1 High Street, o.t. (1803)

JOHN COLEMAN, cabinetmaker, 28 Pitt Street, o.t., shop, South Street (1802, 1803) ; Aisquith Street, o.t. (1810) ; northeast corner of Sharp Street and German Lane, dwelling, 256 Baltimore Street (1822-23)

COLEMAN & TAYLOR, cabinetmakers, 51 South Street, shop, 36 Water Street (1800-01, 1802, 1803, 1804) ; 34 N. Gay Street (1807, 1808)

EDWARD COLEY, cabinetmaker, Guilford Alley, north side west of Light Street (1827) ; W. Falls Avenue (1831) ; Wilk Street 1 door West of Canal Street (1840)

GREENBURY COLLINS, cabinetmaker, York Street, f.h. (1817-18) ; Guilford Alley, f.h. (1819) ; Sugar Alley, south side east of Goodman Street (1822-23) ; Forrest Street, west side south of Sugar Alley, f.h. (1824) ; Montgomery Street, south side east of Charles (1827)

JAMES COLLINS, cabinetmaker, Light Street north of Montgomery (1831)

COMBS & JENKINS, cabinetmakers, 18 Light Street (1802)

THOMAS COMBS, cabinetmaker, 47 Water Street (1803) ; 48 South Street (1804)

*CHARLES COMMON, carver and gilder, 33 S. Calvert Street (1829)

JAMES CONNELLY, cabinetmaker, Harford Avenue, o.t. (1829)

JOHN CONROD/CONRAD, windsor chairmaker, 41 N. Gay Street (1802, 1804) ; shop, Pratt Street, dwelling, 43 S. Gay Street (1803) ; chairmaker, 41 N. Gay Street (1807, 1808) ; chair manufactory, 41 N. Gay Street (1810) ; chairmaker, 43 N. Gay Street (1814-15, 1816)

COLUMBUS E. COOK, furniture warehouse, Baltimore and Harrison Streets (1822-23, 1827, 1831, 1833)

JOHN H. COOK, cabinetmaker, intersection of Howard and Liberty Streets (1824, 1827, 1831, 1833, 1835, 1837)

THOMAS COOK, cabinetmaker, William Street (1833, 1835)

WASHINGTON COOK, furniture warehouse, 20 E. Baltimore Street (1827)

WILLIAM COOK, cabinetmaker, Bond Street, f.p. (1802) ; 2 Shakespeare Street (1804) ; furniture store, 8 Market Space (1819, 1822-23) ; 28 E. Baltimore Street (1827, 1831, 1833)

WILLIAM COOK & COMPANY, cabinetmakers, 45 Bond Street, f.p. (1803)

EDWARD COOLER/COOLEY, cabinetmaker, Forrest Lane near Conewago Street (1816) ; Pearl Street east side south of Bath (1822-23) ; Busy Alley, south side west of Goodman Street, f.h. (1824)

HADAWAY COOPER, cabinetmaker, Hill Street near Light (1833) ; Pennsylvania Avenue north of Franklin Street (1835)

VINCENT COOPER, chairmaker, 13 Cheapside (1802, 1803)

HENRY COPEMAN, cabinetmaker, 81 Pratt Street (1837)

DAVID COPPERSMITH, cabinetmaker, Franklin Street east of Cove (1837, 1840)

WILLIAM CORNTHWAIT, cabinetmaker, 119 Bond Street, f.p. (1808) ; 106 corner of Bond and Fleet Streets, f.p. (1810, 1814-15, 1816, 1817-18) ; Straight Lane, north side east of Lloyd Street (1822-23, 1824) ; 26 Fleet Street (1827) ; 29 Fleet Street (1829, 1831, 1833, 1835, 1837, 1840)

JAMES C. COWARDING, cabinetmaker, 36 S. High Street (1833, 1835) ; 7 Mott Street (1840)

NATHANIEL COX, cabinetmaker, corner of Eutaw and Mulberry Streets (1840)

SAMUEL N. COX, cabinetmaker, Liberty Street (1822-23, 1824) ; East Street (1827, 1829)

DAVID COYLE, cabinetmaker, Franklin Street near Reisterstown Road (1817-18) ; Franklin Street near Green (1819) ; southwest corner of Fayette and Green Streets (1822-23) ; Back Street south of Hamburg, f.h. (1824) ; Johnson Street, east side (1827) ; Hill Street east of Charles (1829) ; Peace Alley east of Paca Street (1831)

ROBERT CRAGGS, JR., cabinetmaker, Pratt Street west of Albemarle (1835)

b

JACOB CRAMWELL, cabinetmaker, Orleans Street 4 doors east of Aisquith (1835)

THOMAS CRAY, cabinetmaker, north side of Conway Street near Howard (1831, 1833) ; 82 Conway Street (1837, 1840)

JAMES CREAGH, cabinetmaker, 5 Green Street (1822-23) ; 49 Water Street, dwelling, Exeter Street south of Pratt (1827)

THOMAS CROCKETT, chairmaker, 14 East Street (1837) ; Sharp Street south of Conway (1840)

THOMAS CROMWELL, cabinetmaker, 12 Thames Street (1833, 1835) ; 26 Thames Street (1837, 1840)

THOMAS CROOK, cabinetmaker, William Street near Watchman and Bratt's foundry, f.h. (1829)

WALTER CROOK, cabinetmaker, 47 St. Patrick's Row (1800-01) ; 47 Market Space (1802, 1803, 1804, 1807, 1808) ; 47 St. Patrick's Row (1810, 1814-15, 1816, 1817-18, 1819) ; 47 Marsh Market Space (1822-23, 1824)

THOMAS CROW, windsor chairmaker, 3 Lancaster Street, f.p. (1802, 1803, 1804) ; chairmaker, 14 Shakespeare Street, f.p. (1807, 1808) ; 11 corner of Shakespeare Street and Apple Alley, f.p. (1810) ; High Street, o.t. (1814-15) ; Fleet near Market Street, f.p. (1816)

ISAAC CRUSOE, cabinetmaker, 5 Saratoga Street (1835)

MARTIN CULBERTSON, cabinetmaker, Saratoga Street between Paca and Green Streets (1835)

DANIEL CUNNINGHAM, cabinetmaker, Maiden Lane near East Street (1831) ; 10 Frederick Street (1833)

LEWIS CURLETT/CURLET, chairmaker, Gay Street west of Aisquith (1835) ; cabinetmaker, 199 N. Gay Street (1837)

ROBERT CURRY, cabinetmaker, rear of 22 N. High Street (1837)

WILLIAM CURTIS, chairmaker, 82 Granby Street, o.t. (1817-18) ; Brandy Alley near Eutaw (1819)

BARTHOLEMEW CUTLIP, cabinetmaker, Lombard Street west of Howard (1833)

ELIJAH DAILEY, chairmaker, Gay Street north of Monument (1840)

ANDREW DALEY ,chairmaker, Exeter Street near Water (1833)

BENJAMIN D. DALEY, japanner, corner of N. Exeter Street and Necessity Alley (1837, 1840)

*JACOB DALEY, chairmaker, Jones or French Street (along Falls) (1804) ; 2 Baltimore Street, dwelling, 68 Front Street, o.t. (1807, 1808) ; 1 Baltimore Street (1810, 1814-15) ; dwelling, 49 Front Street (1816) ; fancy chair factory, 1 Baltimore Street, dwelling, 49 Front Street, o.t. (1817-18, 1819) ; chairmaker, Baltimore Street (1822-23) ; dwelling, King George Street, north side east of Albemarle, o.t. (1824) ; dwelling, E. Water Street, north side west of High (1827) ; chair factory, Baltimore Street bridge (1833) ; glass store, 2nd story of Bazaar, dwelling, 12 Harrison Street, chair factory, Baltimore Street at the bridge (1835) ; W. Baltimore Street on the Falls, dwelling, Harrison Street adjoining Bazaar (1837, 1840)

JACOB DALEY & SON, chair factor, E. Baltimore Street, north side adjoining the bridge, dwelling, Water Street, north side west of High, o.t. (1829) ; chairmakers, Baltimore Street at the bridge, dwelling, corner of Albemarle and E. Water Streets (1831, 1833)

JACOB DALEY, JR., chairmaker, Baltimore Street 2nd door from Eden (1840)

JOSEPH DALEY, chairmaker, 34 Lombard Street east of Frederick (1840)

CHARLES DARAGA, cabinetmaker, 98 Bond Street, f.p. (1817-18)

DAVID DAVENPORT, cabinetmaker, 5 N. Liberty Street, dwelling, Liberty Street, east side south of German (1822-23) ; cabinet and chairmaker, 3 N. Liberty Street, dwelling, North Street, east side south of Lexington (1824) ; cabinetmaker, E. Baltimore Street, south side near Harford Run (1827)

LEWIS DAVENPORT, cabinetmaker, Great York Street near Harford Run, o.t. (1819) ; dwelling, northwest corner of Dulany and Caroline Streets, o.t. (1824) ; dwelling, Great York Street, south side west of Harford Run (1827) ; cabinetmaker, E. Baltimore Street west of Harford Run, o.t. (1829, 1833)

DAVENPORT & MARSH, cabinetmakers, Great York Street, south side west of Harford Run, o.t. (1822-23, 1814) ; E. Baltimore Street near Canal (1831)

HENRY DAVID, cabinetmaker, 95 E. Fleet Street, f.p. (1817-18)

JAMES DAVIDSON, cabinetmaker, 1 Baltimore Street (1800-01, 1802, 1803) ; 3 Baltimore Street (1804) ; also listed at 1 Pratt Street (1802)

ROBERT DAVIDSON, chairmaker, 14 Pitt Street, o.t. (1802, 1803, 1810, 1817-18, 1819) ; rush bottom chairmaker, near 12 Pitt Street, o.t. (1804)

*DAVID DAVIS, fancy chairmaker, 5 Lexington Street (1819) ; cabinet and chairmaker, Pratt Street, south side west of Hanover (1822-23) ; ornamental painter, E. Baltimore Street west of High, dwelling, Potter Street east of Gay, o.t. (1829)

JAMES DAVIS, furniture store, 14 Market Space (1816, 1817-18)

ROBERT DAVIS, JR., chairmaker, McElderry Street, o.t. (1807, 1808)

WILLIAM DAVIS, cabinetmaker, northeast corner of Eutaw Street and Dutch Alley, dwelling, Hanover Street, east side north of Uhler's Alley (1822-23)

HENRY DAVY, cabinetmaker, E. Fleet Street near Wolf (1804) ; 95 E. Fleet Street, f.p. (1810, 1814-15, 1816, 1819, 1822-23, 1824, 1827, 1829, 1833, 1835, 1837, 1840)

ISAAC DAWSON, cabinetmaker, 101 Hanover Street (1829)

WILLIAM DAY, cabinetmaker, 4 Ross Street (1833)

*JAMES DEBAUFRE/DEBOFFRA, coach painter, 49 N. Frederick Street (1819) ; coach and ornamental painter, shop, 23 Harrison Street, dwelling, 23 Pitt Street (1829)

*CORNELIUS DeBEET/DeBREET, fancy painter, 17 Harrison Street (1810) ; Mulberry Street, corner of Lerew's Alley (1812) ; painter, Holliday Street near Pleasant (1819) ; ornamental painter, Pitt Street east of Front, o.t. (1829) ; fancy painter, 14 Pitt Street (1831) ; painter, 14 Pitt Street (1833) ; ornamental painter, 14 Pitt Street (1835) ; painter, 14 Pitt Street (1837, 1840)

BARTHOLOMEW DEGOEY, furniture store, 69 Harrison Street (1840)

CHARLES DEHEREGUY, cabinetmaker, Gough Street, south side of Carolina, f.p. (1822-23) ; 98 Caroline, f.p. (1824)

*JOHN DELPHEY/DELPHINE/DELPHIA, orna-mental painter, southwest corner of Wolf and Gough Streets, f.p. (1824) ; chair ornamenter, east side north of Pitt Street (1827) ; ornamental painter, Spring Street near E. Pratt, f.p. (1829) ; chair ornamenter, Potter Street near Douglass (1831)

ORLANDO DELPHEY, cabinetmaker, 101 Bond Street (1835)

PETER DEL VECCHIO, print and looking glass store, 1 S. Calvert Street (1808) ; carver and gilder, 3 S. Calvert Street (1814-15) ; carver, gilder, picture frame maker, looking glass and print seller, 3 S. Calvert Street (1816) ; carver and gilder, 7 S. Howard Street (1819)

CHARLES DEMANGIN, cabinetmaker, 58 Charles Street (1800-01, 1802, 1803, 1804) ; 103 N. Howard Street (1807, 1808, 1810, 1814-15, 1816) ; 88 N. Howard Street (1812)

d

LEWIS DEMOIRCE, cabinetmaker, Prince Street, north side east of Bishop's Alley, f.p. (1822-23)

JOHN DEMPSEY, chairmaker, North Street near Bridge, o.t. (1816)

JOHN DENMEAD, cabinet and chairmaker, 66 South Street, dwelling, Conewago Street (1802, 1803, 1808); 62 South Street (1810)

DENMEAD & KELLEY, cabinetmakers, 3 Light Street (1804)

JACOB DENNIS, cabinetmaker, Union Street south of Ross (1837)

JOHN DENSON, cabinetmaker, Hawk Street west of Concord (1840)

CHARLES DEVEREL, cabinetmaker, Argyle Alley near Aliceanna Street, f.p. (1819)

JOHN DICKENSON, carver and gilder, Aisquith Street south of McElderry, o.t. (1819)

HENRY O. DIFFENDERFFER, cabinetmaker, Water Street east of Exeter (1835, 1837)

WILLIAM DILEHUNT, cabinetmaker, Orleans Street west of Aisquith (1837)

PAULUS DIMAL, cabinetmaker, Hillen Street east of Potter (1840)

SAMUEL DINSMORE, cabinet warehouse, 5 S. Frederick Street (1817-18)

MATTHEW DOBSON, cabinetmaker, Milk Lane, o.t. (1817-18); 22 Water Street, workshop, 5 Second Street (1819, 1822-23); 32 Water Street (1824)

ALBERT DONOVAN, cabinetmaker, Hillen Street near East, o.t. (1829, 1831, 1835)

EDWARD DORSEY, cabinetmaker, 4 Market Space (1810)

HENRY K. DORSEY/HENRY H. DORSEY, cabinetmaker, 11 Union Street, o.t. (1812); Forrest Lane (1817-18); corner of Saratoga Street and Forrest Lane (1819, 1822-23, 1824); 22 New Church Street (1827, 1829); 55 Wagon Alley (1831, 1833); 45 N. Sharp Street (1835); also listed at 95 Fleet Street (1835); Park Street south of Lexington (1840)

JOHN DOUGHERTY, cabinetmaker, New Church Street (1800-01, 1802, 1803, 1804, 1807, 1808)

RISDON DOWNEY, chairmaker, French Street north of Potter, o.t. (1829); Forrest Street near Gay (1831); N. Exeter Street near French (1833); Frederick Street near Gay (1835)

*ERNEST DREYER, painter of decoration, 266 Howard Street north of Madison (1840)

NATHANIEL DRIGGS, japanner, lower end of Potter Street, o.t. (1817-18)

JOHN H. DRYDEN, cabinetmaker, 19 Comet Street west of Aisquith (1827)

FRANCIS DUBLIN, cabinetmaker, Holliday Street (1817-18)

AIME DUBOIS, cabinetmaker, 35 S. Gay Street (1810); 51 Water Street (1814-15); 98 Bond Street, f.p. (1816)

JACOB DUBOIS, cabinetmaker, 98 Bond Street, f.p. (1817-18)

JAMES DUDDELL, cabinetmaker, 53 N. Gay Street (1812); Green Street, east side north of North, o.t. (1824); Paca Street, east side north of Lexington (1827); 58 Pennsylvania Avenue (1831); 44 Pennsylvania Avenue (1833); Pennsylvania Avenue north of St. Mary Street (1835, 1837, 1840)

HENRY DUKEHART, furniture store, 58 Baltimore Street, dwelling, 5 Front Street (1831, 1833); cabinet manufactory, 24 Harrison Street (1835)

WILLIAM DUNARGEIN, cabinetmaker, 62 S. Charles Street (1802)

JOHN DUNMEAD, cabinetmaker, dwelling, Conewago Street (1802)

JAMES DUNN, cabinetmaker, 124 Wolf Street, f.p. (1817-18); Pleasant Street west of North (1840)

e

f

PEARL DURKEE, cabinetmaker, Pitt Street 3 doors from Aisquith (1837, 1840)

STEPHEN S. K. DURKEE, cabinetmaker, 6 Water Street west of South (1831) ; 82 Harrison Street (1833)

JOHN DUTTON, cabinetmaker, Apple Alley near German Street, f.p. (1817-18)

ROBERT DUTTON, cabinetmaker, Lee Street near Hughes' quay (1817-18) ; 98 Bond Street, f.p. (1819, 1822-23, 1824, 1827, 1829, 1831, 1833) ; wareroom, 124 Bond Street (1831) ; cabinetmaker, 21 Fleet Street east of Bond (1840)

J. F. DUVIVIER, sign painter, 87 French Street (1802)

W. DYER, chairmaker, rear of St. Paul Street near Hamilton (1829)

JAMES S. DYKES, chairmaker, 74 S. Howard Street (1824)

EANERGEY & CO., cabinetmakers, 29 Bond Street, f.p. (1803)

J. EARENGEY, cabinetmaker, shop, 29 Bond Street (1804)

FREDERICK EARING, chairmaker, York Avenue, west side north of Madison, o.t. (1824)

EDWARD EARLY, cabinetmaker, Duke Street, west side south of Harford Run (1822-23)

WILLIAM EARNEST, cabinetmaker, 17 Harrison Street (1840)

EASTWOOD & MARSH, cabinetmakers, 27 E. Baltimore Street (1837) ; 25 E. Baltimore Street, dwelling, 73 E. Lombard Street (1840)

EDMONDSON & FREELAND, cabinetmakers and upholsterers, 62 South Street; dwelling, Eli Edmondson, E. Pratt Street, f.p. (1831)

*J. EDMONDSON, ornamental painter, 11 Commerce Street (1829)

JAMES EDMONDSON, chairmaker, Park Street, east side south of Lexington (1827)

CHARLES EDWARDS, cabinetmaker, Hill Street, f.h. (1817-18)

HENRY EDWARDS, cabinetmaker, 174 N. High Street (1827) ; 136 N. Exeter Street (1829) ; southeast corner of Orleans Street and Long Lane (1831) ; 80 Harrison Street (1835) ; cabinet wareroom, 90 Harrison Street (1837, 1840)

LEROY EDWARDS, cabinetmaker, Front Street north of York (1835)

A. & D. EGAN, cabinetmakers, 89 W. Pratt Street (1833)

DANIEL EGAN, cabinetmaker, Camden Street east of Paca (1840)

JOHN EHRENMAN, chairmaker, Frenchman's Alley (1810)

CHARLES EICOFF, cabinetmaker, corner of Constitution and Falls Streets (1840)

J. EIHRMAN, chairmaker, Uhler's Alley off Hanover Street (1804)

HILLARY I. ELDER, cabinetmaker, Cove Street south of Franklin (1840)

ERICK ELEASON, furniture store, corner of Howard Street and Wagon Alley (1833) ; 42 W. Franklin Street (1831)

JOHN ELLIOTT, cabinetmaker, corner of Green and North Streets, o.t. (1817-18)

WILLIAM ELVIES, cabinetmaker, Goldsborough Street (1800-01)

NICHOLAS EMICH, cabinetmaker, Baltimore Street west of Pearl (1835, 1837)

*GEORGE ENDICOTT, ornamental painter, northwest corner of Charles and Baltimore Streets, dwelling, Conway Street near Charles (1829)

g

GEORGE ENSINGER, cabinetmaker, Apple Alley north of Shakespeare Street (1830)

ERENGEY & COOK, cabinetmakers, 11 Bond Street, f.p. (1802)

BARTHOLOMEW ESPIET, cabinetmaker, 33 S. Charles Street (1812)

JOHN ETSCHBERGER, cabinet and chairmaker, 49 South Street (1814-15)

*ETSCHBERGER & STAMMEN, fancy chair factory, 49 Water Street, corner of S. Gay (1817-18)

GEORGE W. EVANS, cabinetmaker, Comet Street, o.t. (1814-15) ; Straight Lane, o.t. (1816) ; Conway Street near Howard (1817-18) ; New Orleans Street near Aisquith (1819) ; piano forte maker, Short Street, east side south of Jefferson (1822-23) ; cabinetmaker, N. Gay Street near East (1831) ; 62 N. Gay Street (1833)

JOHN EVANS, cabinetmaker, Friendship Street, east side north of McElderry, o.t. (1824)

WILLIAM FARIS, cabinetmaker, 38 Calvert Street (1800-01) ; carver, gilder and looking glass manufacturer, corner of S. Charles Street and Uhler's Alley (1802, 1803)

JOHN FARSON, cabinetmaker, 24 N. Gay Street (1831) ; 6 Gay Street (1833) ; Pratt Street 3rd house east of bridge (1835)

JOSEPH FAVE, looking glass manufactory, 51 N. Gay Street (1814-15)

*ELISHA/ELIJAH FENNELL, ornamental painter, Liberty Street, o.t. (1817-18) ; 19 Potter Street, o.t. (1824) ; chair painter, Forrest Street near Maryland Penitentiary (1831)

L. FINKER, cabinetmaker, Peace Alley near Howard Street (1831)

*HUGH FINLAY/FINLEY, dwelling, 32 N. Gay Street (1819) ; fancy furniture warehouse, 32 N. Gay Street, dwelling, 34 N. Gay Street (1822, 1824, 1827)

*HUGH FINLAY & CO., fancy furniture warehouse, 32 N. Gay Street (1817-18) ; fancy chair factors, 32 N. Gay Street (1829)

*JOHN FINLAY/FINLEY, painter, dwelling and shop, S. Frederick Street (1800-01) ; coach painter, shop, S. Frederick Street, dwelling, Harrison Street (1802) ; fancy chair warehouse, 34 N. Gay Street, dwelling, 32 N. Gay Street (1814-15) ; warehouse, 32 N. Gay Street, dwelling, 34 N. Gay Street (1816) ; warehouse, 32 N. Gay Street, dwelling, Pleasant Street near St. Paul's Lane (1817-18, 1819) ; chairmaker, N. Gay Street, dwelling, 2 Lexington Street, north side west of North (1827) ; coachmaker, 30 N. Gay Street (1829) ; coach and fancy chair manufacturer, 21 N. Gay Street, dwelling, 34 N. Gay Street (1831) ; chairmaker, 32 N. Gay Street, dwelling, 34 N. Gay Street (1835, 1837)

*JOHN FINLAY & CO., furniture store, 32 N. Gay Street (1833)

*JOHN & HUGH FINLAY/FINLEY, painters, S. Frederick Street, dwelling, Harrison Street (1803) ; fancy chairmakers, 190 Baltimore Street near N. Charles (1804) ; coachmakers, 22 S. Frederick Street (1804) ; fancy chairmakers, 60 N. Gay Street (1807) ; fancy furniture manufacturers, 60 corner of Gay and Frederick Streets (1810, 1812) ; fancy furniture warehouse, 32 N. Gay Street (1819)

JAMES FINNEGAN, cabinetmaker, Park Street west side north of Lexington (1827)

LEWIS FINNY, cabinetmaker, 24 Great York, o.t. (1819)

DOMINICK FIQUET, cabinetmaker, Guilford Alley, f.h. (1817-18)

HENRY M. FISHER, carver and gilder, 30 Marsh Market Space (1824)

*ROBERT FISHER, chairmaker, shop under 35 S. Gay Street (1800-01) ; 50 N. Gay Street (1802) ; fancy chairmaker, shop, S. Gay Street, dwelling, 46 Jones Street, o.t. (1803) ; chairmaker, 37 S. Gay Street, dwelling, Jones Street, o.t. (1807, 1808) ; chairmaker, 37 S. Gay Street, dwelling, 46 James Street, o.t. (1810)

WILLIAM FISHER, chairmaker, Jones Street, o.t. (1803, 1804)

STERN FLEMING, cabinetmaker, 41 Fleet Street, f.p. (1803)

MR. FOGLESTON, cabinetmaker, 18 Mercer Street (1835)

JOHN FOLEY, cabinetmaker, S. Frederick Street (1800-01)

TIMOTHY FOLEY, cabinetmaker, 7 Water Street (1807) ; 98 High Street, o.t. (1812) ; Salisbury Street, o.t. (1814-15) ; Thames Street near Bond, f.p. (1816) ; 32 Granby Street, o.t. (1817-18) ; 1 Friendship Street, o.t. (1819) ; 116 Bond Street, f.p. (1822-23) ; 19 Caroline Street, f.p. (1824) ; Forrest Street west side north of Douglass (1827, 1829) ; northeast corner of Ann and Aliceanna Streets (1831)

WILLIAM FOLSANKS, cabinetmaker, corner of Mercer and Grant Streets (1837)

JOHN FORD, cabinetmaker, over 10 W. Water Street (1831)

RALPH E. FORRESTER, cabinetmaker, 32 Water Street (1814-15) ; 61 St. Patrick's Row (1816, 1817-18) ; 61 Market Space (1819, 1822-23) ; N. Howard Street near Richmond (1827, 1829)

FORRESTER & WHEELER, cabinetmakers, Water Street, o.t. (1812)

FOSS & FOWLES, cabinetmakers, corner of Howard and Saratoga Streets (1833)

HENRY J. FOSS, cabinet and chairmaker, 10 S. Frederick Street (1835)

WILLIAM W. FOSS, cabinetmaker, Hill Street near Hanover (1835)

LEONARD FRAILEY, japanner, over No. 1 S. Eutaw Street (1835)

JOHN F. FRASH, cabinetmaker, William Street south of Warren (1831)

ROBERT FREDERICK, chairmaker, Aisquith Street, east side south of N. Gay (1827, 1839, 1831) ; N. Gay Street south of Mott (1833, 1835) ; corner of Potter and Gay Streets (1837) ; Gay Street near engine house (1840)

WILLIAM FREEMAN, cabinetmaker, 120 Bond Street, f.p. (1802) ; Lancaster Street, dwelling, 61 Ann Street, f.p. (1810) ; Argyle Alley, f.p. (1812) ; 10 Aliceanna Street, f.p. (1814-15) ; 124 Wolf Street, f.p. (1817-18)

SAMUEL FREY, cabinetmaker, Pearl Street north of Lexington (1837, 1840)

*ELIJAH FREYER, gilder, 67 E. Baltimore Street near Canal (1833)

WILLIAM FRIETCHLER, cabinetmaker, Franklin Street east of Paca (1835)

NIMROD FRUM, cabinetmaker, Eden Street south of Gough (1831, 1833) ; 1 Block Street (1835)

BENEDICT FUNCK, cabinetmaker, southeast corner of New Lane and Long Alley (1824)

JOHN GAINNIER, cabinetmaker, N. Charles Street (1800-01, 1802)

WILLIAM GAMBEL, cabinetmaker, corner of Water and Gay Streets (1829, 1831, 1833)

ROBERT GAMBLE, chairmaker, corner of Water and Grant Streets (1831) ; Lee Street west of Sharp (1837)

ROBERT GAMBRALL, chairmaker, Forrest Street 1 door north of Ensor (1840)

FRANCIS GARDINER, auction furniture store, Second Street between Gay and Frederick (1833)

PETER GARDINER, chairmaker, 7 Bank Street (1814-15)

*JOHN M. GARDNER, house, sign and ornamental painter, northwest corner of Baltimore and North Streets, dwelling, corner of Fayette and Pearl Streets (1840)

PETER GARDNER, chairmaker, 61 Harrison Street (1810) ; Low Street, o.t. (1812, 1817-18)

h

JAMES GAREN, chairmaker, Hampstead Street east of Eden (1840)

JAMES GARING, chairmaker, Park Street, west side north of Lexington (1827)

FRANCIS B. GARISH, ebonist, 53 High Street, o.t. (1803) ; 82 High Street, o.t. (1810) ; piano forte maker, 82 High Street, o.t. (1817-18)

JOHN B. GARISH, piano forte maker, 82 High Street, o.t. (1819)

RICHARD GARRET, cabinetmaker, Aliceanna Street (1827)

JOHN GARRETT, cabinetmaker, 11 Aliceanna Street, f.p. (1829, 1833, 1837) ; 9 Aliceanna Street (1831, 1840) ; Aliceanna Street east of Market Street (1835)

SAMUEL GARRETT, cabinetmaker, Orleans Street west of Aisquith (1831) ; Lancaster Street near Argyle Alley (1833)

JAMES GARRING/GARING/GARRON, chairmaker, Sharp Street near Lee (1829, 1831, 1833)

JAMES GARY, chairmaker, Mulliken Street west of Strawberry Alley (1837)

JAMES GAW, cabinetmaker, 88 Harrison Street, dwelling, 53 Harrison Street (1822-23)

GEORGE GEDDES, cabinetmaker, Mulliken Street east of Caroline (1835)

JACOB GERBER, cabinetmaker, rear of Union Street east of Pennsylvania Avenue (1829)

DAVID GERLAN, chairmaker, 47 Green Street, o.t. (1819)

JOB GERMAN, chairmaker, E. Baltimore Street east of Eden (1837)

*JONATHAN GERMAN, ornamental painter, Green Street north of Pitt and Front, near Ploughman, o.t. (1819) ; Baltimore Street at Falls Bridge (1831) ; dwelling, Exeter Street near Necessity Alley (1829, 1831, 1835)

*GILL & ROSS, fancy chair and cabinetmakers, 8 Hanover Street (1829)

*BRYSON GILL, fancy chair factory, 8 Hanover Street, dwelling, 29 Harrison Street (1824, 1827)

GUSTAVUS GILES, cabinetmaker, Charles Street 2 doors south of Lee (1840)

STEPHEN GILLESPIE, cabinetmaker, Fayette and Holliday Streets (1829, 1833, 1835, 1837, 1840)

CHARLES GIST, cabinetmaker, Camden Street near Paca (1819)

JOSEPH GLICK, cabinetmaker, 21 Crook's Row, Monument Street (1840)

LEWIS GLUCK, cabinetmaker, Pennsylvania Avenue north of Hoffman Street (1835)

*GEORGE GOFORTH, gilder and sign painter, 45 Bridge Street, o.t. (1812)

*JOHN GOLDRICH, carver and gilder, 40 N. Frederick Street (1814-15)

GORDON & SMITH, chairmakers, 49 South Street (1831)

JOHN H. GORDON, chairmaker, 11 Second Street (1831) ; chairmaker and grocer, southeast corner of Water and South Streets (1833, 1835) ; 73 Water Street (1837)

W. GORDON, chair manufacturer, corner of Water and South Streets, dwelling, Gough Street (1837)

WILLIAM GORDON, chairmaker, precincts beyond Bridge Street (1802)

PETER GORET, cabinetmaker, 33 S. Charles Street (1807, 1808) ; joiner and cabinetmaker, 31 S. Charles Street (1810)

GEORGE GORRELL, chairmaker, Salisbury Street between Exeter and High, dwelling, Caroline Street south of Pratt (1840)

KARL GOTTLIEB, cabinetmaker, Baltimore Street east of Pine (1833)

FREDERICK GRAHAM, cabinetmaker, 13 Light Street (1800-01, 1802)

HUGH GRAHAM, cabinetmaker, Lee Street east of Charles (1831) ; Charles Street near Hill (1835) ; Charles Street south of Busy Alley (1837)

GEORGE W. GREEN, chairmaker, 31 S. Calvert Street (1812) ; 56 Front Street, o.t. (1816) ; 44 N. Frederick Street (1817-18) ; Pine Street south of Franklin (1819) ; southwest corner of Cheapside and Water Streets (1824) ; E. Centre Street, south side adjoining bridge (1827) ; Front Street near Hillen, o.t. (1829, 1831) ; N. Eden Street near Hampstead (1833)

JOHN GREEN, cabinetmaker, Wagon Alley between Eutaw and Lexington Streets (1804)

PETER GREEN, cabinetmaker, Forrest Street east of Aisquith (1840)

HENRY GREENY, piano forte maker, 3 East Street (1824)

JOHN GREGO/GRIGO & CO., looking glass manufacturer, 26 South Street (1803, 1804)

GREIVE & GORDON, piano forte manufactory, 3 East Street (1819)

HENRY W. GREWE, piano forte maker, 1 East Street (1814-15)

JAMES GRIFFIS/GRIFFISS, cabinetmaker, Ensor Street, foot of Gallow's Hill (1837) ; 141 High Street south of Hillen (1840)

MOSES GRIST, cabinetmaker, Pratt Street 4 doors east of Spring (1835)

HENRY GROFF, cabinetmaker, 19 N. Gay Street (1800-01) ; Fish Street (1802, 1804)

GROFF & MEGGS, cabinetmakers, 30 N. Gay Street (1807, 1808)

JESSE GUDGEON, cabinetmaker, southeast corner of Bond and Fleet Streets and grocer, 106 Bond Street (1831)

CHARLES GUEST, cabinetmaker, Union Street, north side east of Pennsylvania Avenue (1822-23)

FRANCIS GUIGNARD, cabinetmaker, S. Frederick Street (1810)

JACOB GUYER, cabinetmaker, Market Street near Thames (1831)

FRANCIS GYBERT, cabinetmaker, Chattsworth Street, north of Saratoga (1837)

GABRIEL HADDICK, cabinetmaker, Petticoat Alley, f.p. (1803)

WILLIAM HALE, cabinetmaker, Harford Road south of Baltimore Street, o.t. (1829)

HENRY HALEY, chairmaker, Aisquith Street near McElderry, o.t. (1816) ; Carolina Street, west side north of Dulaney (1822-23)

EDWARD HALL, cabinetmaker, Potter Street, o.t. (1804)

*JAMES E. HALL, chair gilder, Charles Street Court north of Camden (1837) ; 45 Charles Street (1840)

JAMES R. HALL, cabinetmaker, 70 King George Street (1822-23)

JOHN HALL, cabinetmaker, 39½ Howard Street (1840)

JOHN B. HALL, cabinetmaker, 30 S. Howard Street (1804) ; corner of South and Water Streets (1807, 1808) ; 32 Granby Street, o.t. (1810) ; 4 Granby Street (1814-15, 1817-18) ; cabinetmaker and captain of the City Watch, dwelling, 6 Granby Street, f.p. (1819, 1822-23, 1824)

WILLIAM HALL, cabinetmaker, 57 Albemarle Street (1833)

WILLIAM L. HAMELL/HAMMELL, cabinetmaker, Prince Street, north side near Exeter, o.t. (1824) ; 1 Camden Street east of Sharp (1827)

WILLIAM F. HAMILL, cabinetmaker, 28 German Street, dwelling, rear of 26 German Street (1831) ; 30 German Street (1833) ; Howard Street 2 doors south of Conway (1840)

GEORGE HAMILTON, cabinetmaker, Fleet Street, f.p. (1800-01)

*JAMES B. HAMILTON, ornamental painter, Dulany Street, south side east of Bond, o.t. (1824) ; 42 Center Market Space (1827, 1829)

JOHN HAMILTON, cabinet furniture store, 8 E. Baltimore Street (1827) ; cabinet and chairmaker, 8 E. Baltimore Street (1829) ; cabinetmaker, 8 E. Baltimore Street (1831)

ROBERT HAMILTON, cabinetmaker, 33 Camden Street east of Hanover (1840)

*JAMES HAMMILL, gilder, Biddle Street (1817-18)

CALEB HANNAH, chairmaker, shop, Fish Market Street and 12 Cheapside, dwelling, 25 Market Space (1800-01, 1802, 1803, 1804)

HIRAM HARDING, cabinetmaker and house joiner, Britton Street near Harford Avenue (1824)

WILLIAM HARE, chairmaker, 66 Front Street, o.t. (1817-18)

GEORGE HARFORD, cabinetmaker, 21 Fleet Street (1835)

JOHN HARPER, piano forte maker, 78 South Street (1804)

WILLIAM HARPER, piano forte maker, 36 N. Frederick Street (1804)

PETER HARR, cabinetmaker, lieutenant of the city watch (1819) ; Duke Street, south side west of Wolf (1822-23) ; Constitution Street near French (1829)

ALFRED C. HARRIS, cabinetmaker, Montgomery Street west of Light (1837, 1840)

JOHN HARRIS, cabinetmaker, 106 Sharp Street (1824) ; York Street east of Charles (1827)

WILLIAM HARRIS, cabinetmaker, 39 N. Gay Street (1800-01, 1803) ; 28 & 29 N. Gay Street (1802) ; shop, 35 N. Gay, dwelling, 29 Bridge Street (1804)

DANIEL HARRISON, cabinetmaker, 145 Bond Street, f.p. (1802)

i

SABRET HARRISON, chairmaker, Eden Street north of York (1835)

JAMES HARVEY, cabinetmaker, Comet Street west of Aisquith (1837)

JOHN W. HASWELL, cabinetmaker, Duke Street, o.t. (1814-15) ; 36 Pitt Street, o.t. (1816, 1817-18) ; 44 Potter Street, o.t. (1822-23, 1824) ; 40 Potter Street (1827)

*JOHN HAYS, firm of McDonald & Hays, house, sign and ornamental painter, southeast corner of Conewago and Liberty Streets, dwelling at and proprietor of the Fayette Street Hotel, 22 Fayette Street (1824)

HENRY HEALY, chairmaker, Aisquith Street, o.t. (1817-18) ; High Street, west side north of Great York, o.t. (1824)

HENRY HENDRICKSON, cabinetmaker, Carpenter Alley near Eutaw Street (1835) ; German Street west of Pearl (1837)

————— HENKEL, cabinetmaker, Orchard Street south of Ross (1840)

EDWARD G. HENRIX, cabinetmaker, Orleans Street west of Canal (1837, 1840)

FREDERICK HEROLT, cabinetmaker, Orchard Street south of Ross (1840)

JARRET HEWES, cabinetmaker, Canal Street south of Gough (1835)

HENRY HICKMAN, chairmaker, East Street near Hillen, dwelling, 84 Harrison, o.t. (1822-23, 1824, 1829, 1833, 1837, 1840)

JOHN HILDILEN, furniture store, 49 Harrison Street (1840)

H. J. HILL, cabinetmaker, 64 N. Howard Street (1831)

ROBERT HILL, cabinetmaker, Pratt Street near lower bridge (1812)

*JOSEPH HILLIER, carver, gilder and picture frame maker, 76 Baltimore Street (1819)

THOMAS HINCK, cabinetmaker, 116 Sharp Street (1827)

THOMAS HINES, cabinetmaker, 52 Camden Street (1810)

THOMAS HINKS, cabinetmaker, 31 Conewago Street (1814-15, 1816)

JOHN HISKEY/HISKY, piano forte manufacturer, 6 S. Calvert Street (1837, 1840)

JOSEPH HISKEY/HISKY, piano forte maker, 7 Water Street (1819) ; northeast corner of Howard and Saratoga Streets (1822-23, 1824, 1827) ; cabinet-maker, Park Street south of Lexington (1833, 1835) ; also listed, piano forte wareroom, over 106 Baltimore Street (1835)

HISS & AUSTEN, cabinetmakers, 23 Fayette Street (1819, 1822-23, 1824, 1827, 1831) ; 69 Fayette Street (1835, 1837, 1840)

*J. L. & J. HISS, fancy chair manufactory, 37 S. Gay Street (1817-18, 1819, 1822-23)

*JACOB HISS/JACOB HISS, JR., fancy chairmaker, 37 S. Gay Street, dwelling, Exeter Street east side south of Queen (1822-23, 1824, 1827, 1829, 1831, 1833, 1835, 1837, 1840)

JESSE L. HISS, chairmaker, 37 S. Gay Street (1816) ; dwelling, Exeter Street, east side south of President's Alley (1822-23) ; cabinet and chairmaker, 18 S. Calvert Street, dwelling, Lloyd Street south of Salisbury, o.t. (1824) ; chairmaker, 9 Temple Street (1827) ; 6 S. Calvert Street (1829, 1831) ; Exeter Street south of Pratt (1837, 1840)

PHILIP HISS, cabinet and chairmaker, 23 Fayette Street, dwelling, 21 Fayette Street (1822-23, 1824) ; dwelling, Courtland Street, east side north of Sara-toga (1827, 1829) ; dwelling, Fayette Street near Howard (1831) ; dwelling, 67 W. Fayette Street (1833)

THOMAS D. HISS, cabinet and chairmaker, 18 S. Calvert Street (1822-23, 1824) ; 6 S. Calvert Street (1829, 1831, 1835) ; furniture factory, 2 Grant Street and 6 S. Calvert Street (1833)

SAMUEL HOBBS, cabinetmaker, King George Street near Pearl (1829, 1831, 1833)

JOHN HODGKINSON, chair factory, Liberty Street, west side north of Baltimore, dwelling, Howard Street west side north of Whiskey Alley (1822-23) ; dwelling, Liberty Street east side near Wagon Alley (1824) ; 32 Hanover Street (1827, 1829, 1831, 1833, 1835, 1837, 1840) ; dwelling, 28 Albemarle Street (1840)

JOHN HOFFMAN, cabinet and chairmaker, 27 Carolina Street, f.p. (1802)

JOHN HOLIDAY, cabinetmaker, Maiden Lane west of Aisquith Street (1835)

JOHN HOLLAND, cabinetmaker, 3 N. Gay Street (1824)

THOMAS H. HOLLINGSWORTH, cabinetmaker, corner of Goodman Street and Honey Alley, f.h. (1817-18)

*HENRY HOOK, house, sign and ornamental painter, 36 . Lexington Street, dwelling, 27 Pearl Street (1819, 1829)

WILLIAM HOOPER, cabinetmaker, Albemarle Street, east side north of E. Pratt (1827)

SOLOMON HOPKINS, cabinetmaker, 76 Liberty Street, o.t. (1817-18) ; Eden Street near German, f.p. (1819) ; Williams Alley, south side east of Spring Street (1822-23)

THOMAS HOPKINS, cabinetmaker, Pratt Street west of Hanover (1829)

G. HORNBY, cabinetmaker, 31 Union Street, o.t. (1800-01, 1802) ; 6 Light Street (1804)

WALTER HORNBY, cabinetmaker, 6 Light Street (1810)

WILLIAM HORNBY, cabinetmaker, 3 Green Street, o.t. (1807) ; 2 O'Donnell's Wharf, dwelling, corner of Mulberry and Green Streets (1808)

WILLIAM HOUSE, chairmaker, Gough Street east of Caroline (1835)

JOHN HOW, carpet and furniture warehouse, 12 S. Calvert Street (1817-18)

PETER HOWLET, cabinetmaker, Potter Street, o.t. (1816)

SAMUEL HOWSER, chairmaker, 19 Pitt Street (1833)

GARRETT HUGHES, cabinetmaker, Hanover Street opposite Meeting House, dwelling, Granby Street east of Gough (1840)

HENRY HUGHES, cabinetmaker, southeast corner of Camden and Charles Streets (1827) ; Welcome Alley west of Charles Street (1829)

JARRAD HUGHES, cabinetmaker, Hanover Street north of Camden (1840)

JOHN HUGHES, cabinetmaker, Aliceanna Street near Argyle Alley (1833) ; corner of Bond and Bank Streets (1837, 1840) ; also listed at Hanover Street north of Camden (1837)

WILLIAM HUGHES, chairmaker, Caroline Street 1 door north of Bank Street (1837)

JOHN HULL, cabinetmaker, 77 Green Street, o.t. (1819)

WILLIAM HUME, cabinetmaker, Sharp Street south of Lexington (1837) ; Forrest Street near Harford Run (1840)

*HENRY C. HUNE, ornamental painter and drawing master, French Street near Bath (1837); Pennsylvania Avenue west of Biddle Street (1840)

JOHN HUNN, cabinetmaker, Harford Avenue south side (1829)

GEORGE HUPPMAN, piano forte maker, S. Sharp Street, west side of Baltimore (1827) ; 20 Light Street (1825, 1837) ; 26 Hanover Street (1840)

JOSEPH HUTTON, cabinetmaker, King George Street, o.t. (1814-15, 1819)

HENRY HUXFORD, japanner, Ferry Road south of Hamburg, f.h. (1824) ; 322 Baltimore Street (1835)

BENJAMIN HYNSON, cabinetmaker, Aisquith Street north of Low (1840)

NATHANIEL HYNSON, cabinetmaker, 98 Bond Street, f.p. (1800-01, 1803, 1804, 1807, 1808, 1810) ; 28 (sic) Bond Street, f.p. (1802)

ALEXANDER INGRAM, chairmaker and painter, Franklin Street near Howard (1810)

j

EDWARD L. IRENMENTEER, chairmaker, corner of Saratoga and Park Streets (1837)

EDWARD IRONMONGER, chairmaker, 26 Lexington Street (1831)

*PETER JACKSON, chair painter, Saratoga Street, south side west of North (1822-23)

*JOSEPH JANVIER, chairmaker, 76 Green Street, o.t. (1814-15, 1816, 1817-18) ; fancy rush bottom chairmaker, 76 Green Street, o.t. (1819, 1822-23) ; chairmaker, 76 Green Street, o.t. (1824) ; 61 Front Street (1827, 1829, 1831)

WILLIAM JEFFERES, chairmaker, Second Street, dwelling, Pitt Street east of Eden (1840)

A. & H. JENKINS, cabinet wareroom, 18 Light Street (1837, 1840)

ANTHONY H. JENKINS, cabinetmaker, 18 Light Street (1833, 1835)

JENKINS & DINSMORE, cabinetmakers, N. Frederick Street between Baltimore and Second (1816)

JAMES JENKINS, cabinet furniture warehouse, upper part of 11 South Street, dwelling, northwest corner of Holliday and Pleasant Streets (1822-23, 1824) ; cabinetmaker, 9 South Street, dwelling, Pratt Street, south side east of High (1827) ; Sugar Alley near S. Charles Street (1833) ; Montgomery Street west of Light (1837)

JAMES & JASON JENKINS, cabinetmakers, 11 and 13 South Street (1819)

MICHAEL JENKINS, cabinetmakers, 18 Light Street (1803, 1804, 1807, 1808, 1810, 1816, 1817-18, 1819, 1822-23, 1824, 1827, 1829, 1831) ; dwelling, 18 Bank Street (1816)

THOMAS JENKINS, chairmaker, Exeter Street north of Baltimore (1835)

JACOB JERBER, cabinetmaker, 42 Park Street (1831)

JOHN JEWELL, chairmaker, Addison Street, o.t. (1812)

HARMKOCH JOHANA, cabinetmaker, corner of Lombard and Liberty Streets (1829)

ISAAC JOHNS, cabinetmaker, Orange Street between Holliday and N. Gay Streets (1800-01)

*ABIJAH JOHNSON, tin-plate worker and japanner, 35 North Street, o.t. (1803) ; ornamental painter, dwelling, Union Street, o.t. (1810) ; japanner, lower end of Potter Street (1817-18)

B. J. JOHNSON, cabinetmaker, 103 N. Howard Street (1824)

EDWARD JOHNSON, chairmaker, near corner of Silver and Pitt Streets (1835)

MRS. EDWARD JOHNSON, chairmaker, near corner of Silver and Pitt Streets (1835)

HOWARD JOHNSON, chairmaker, corner of Bond and Mullikin Streets (1840)

JOHN JOHNSON, cabinetmaker, 10 York Street, f.h. (1837)

WILLIAM JOHNSON, cabinetmaker, Lerew's Alley (1833)

HAMILTON JONES, cabinetmaker, 11 & 13 S. Sharp Street (1833)

JOHN JONES, cabinetmaker, Mott Street, west side (1831)

MAHLER JONES, cabinetmaker, Gillingham's Alley (1819) ; 88 N. Howard Street (1822-23)

ROBERT JONES, chairmaker, East Street north of Pitt (1833)

*WILLIAM JONES, carver, gilder, looking glass and picture frame manufacturer, 42 N. Gay Street (1816)

JOHN JORDAN, cabinetmaker, Potter Street near Low (1829, 1831, 1833, 1835, 1837, 1840)

JOURNEYMEN CABINETMAKERS' WARE

ROOMS, 10 Gay Street south of Baltimore (1840)

ANDREW JUDLAN, cabinetmaker, Liberty Street near McElderry, o.t. (1819)

FREDERICK KARSON, cabinetmaker, Busy Alley near Howard Street (1819)

JOHN KECK, cabinetmaker, N. Gay Street near East (1831)

WILLIAM KEENER, chairmaker, 29 S. Frederick Street (1817-18) ; Water Street (1824) ; 12 Harrison Street (1829, 1831) ; chair factory, 21 Potter Street north of Gay (1833) ; chairmaker, 59 Albemarle Street (1837, 1840)

ISSAC KEMP, cabinetmaker, Baltimore Street east of Cove (1837)

JOHN E. KEMP, cabinetmaker, Park Street south of Lexington (1833)

J. R. KEMP, cabinetmaker, Pennsylvania Avenue north of St. Mary's (1831)

*JOHN H. KENNEDY, chair ornamenter, west side of Caroline Street north of E. Baltimore (1831) ; 24 Gay Street, dwelling, N. Caroline Street (1833) ; fancy chairmaker, 9 N. Gay Street (1835) ; fancy chair manufactory, 8 N. Gay Street (1837, 1840)

MICHAEL KENNEDY, cabinetmaker, 25 Lombard Street west of Center Market Space (1840)

*SAMUEL S. KENNEDY, carver, gilder and looking glass manufacturer, 3 N. Gay Street (1803)

WILLIAM KENNELLY, cabinetmaker, northeast of Monument (1835)

WILLIAM KEPLER, cabinetmaker, west end of Baltimore Street (1835)

JOHN KEREY, cabinetmaker, Brandy Alley near Sharp Street (1819)

WILLIAM KESTEN, cabinetmaker, German Lane west of Charles Street (1824)

GEORGE KESTERSON, cabinetmaker, 45 S. Frederick Street (1817-18) ; 64 Harrison Street, dwelling, Cowpen Alley (1819) ; 14 S. Charles Street (1824)

*JOHN KING, chairmaker, 30 N. Gay Street (1810);
22 N. Gay Street, dwelling, 101 Saratoga Street (1814-15); 24 N. Gay Street, dwelling, 101 Saratoga Street (1816, 1817-18); fancy chair factory, 24 N. Gay Street, dwelling near Carolina, o.t. (1819); chairmaker, 24 N. Gay Street, dwelling, Eutaw Street, east side south of Fayette (1822-23); 24 N. Howard Street, dwelling, Dulaney Street 1 door west of Caroline, f.p. (1824); 24 N. Gay Street, dwelling, Baltimore Street near Caroline (1829)

JOHN F. KING, cabinetmaker, corner of Hillen and Front Streets (1840)

PHILIP KIRCHEST, cabinetmaker, 15 Wilk Street (1837)

JAMES KIRKPATRICK, cabinetmaker, 76 Bond Street, f.p. (1807, 1808)

LEWIS/LUTHER KISTER, cabinetmaker, Baltimore Street east of Cove (1835); Long Alley south of Saratoga Street (1837); Green Street 3 doors south of Baltimore Street (1840)

AUGUSTUS KITTLER, furniture store, 59 Bond Street (1840)

JOSEPH KLUCK, cabinetmaker, Crook's Row, Montgomery Street (1837)

WILLIAM KNABE, piano maker, 45 Light Street (1840)

WILLIAM KNAUF, cabinetmaker, 61 Center Market Space (1840)

*JAMES KNOX, chairmaker, corner of East and Lemmon Streets (1817-18); fancy chairmaker, 31 S. Calvert Street (1819, 1822-23, 1824)

J. H. KOCH, cabinetmaker, northwest corner of Howard and Liberty Streets

JESSE KOSYRE, cabinetmaker, Green Street north of Mulberry (1840)

————— KREBBS, cabinetmaker, 123 S. Sharp Street (1835)

SAMUEL KREBS, cabinetmaker, 72 Hanover Street (1833)

ANTHONY KUHN, cabinetmaker, Pennsylvania Avenue west of Biddle Street (1840)

AARON LANCASTER, cabinetmaker, Jefferson Row, Conway Street (1835)

ANN LANCASTER, cabinetmaker, 10 Camden Street (1837)

JOHN LANCASTER, cabinetmaker, Mercer Street near Light (1835, 1837)

JOHN D. LANCASTER, cabinetmaker, 24 N. Exeter Street (1831)

DAVID LANGLEY, cabinetmaker, Britton Street northeast of Monument (1835)

EDWARD LANGLEY, cabinetmaker, Orleans Street west of Canal (1837, 1840)

SYLVESTER LANGLEY, cabinetmaker, Harford Avenue nearly opposite Greble's Pottery (1831); Holland Street near Canal (1840)

*EDWARD LATHAM, fancy chairmaker, 5 Jones Street, o.t. (1810)

SAMUEL LAUDER/LAWDER, cabinetmaker, Carpenter's Alley (1833); Busy Alley (1835)

WILLIAM LAVELY, cabinetmaker, 28 Pitt Street (1804); 27 Union Street, o.t. (1812); dwelling, Vulcan Alley (1816)

ANTHONY LAW, cabinetmaker, Fayette Street (1800-01, 1802, 1804); corner of Water and South Streets (1807, 1808); 21 Fayette Street, dwelling, 11 Fayette Street (1810, 1814-15, 1816); dwelling, Paca Street near Saratoga (1817-18)

LAW & DENMEAD, cabinet and chairmakers, 66 South Street (1803, 1804)

JOHN LAW, cabinetmaker, 64 South Street (1804)

THOMAS LAW, japanner, Paca Street south of Saratoga (1840)

JOHN LAWSON, cabinetmaker, 61 Harrison Street (1807, 1808)

REUBEN LEAGUE, chairmaker, 32 N. Gay Street (1800-01, 1802); windsor chairmaker, 32 N. Gay Street (1803); chairmaker, 32 N. Gay Street, dwelling, Harrison Street (1804)

JOHN LEATHERBURY, chairmaker, 21 Comet Street (1814-15)

k

THOMAS LEATHERBURY, chairmaker, Straight Lane, o.t. (1814-15) ; Liberty Street near Pitt, o.t. (1816, 1817-18)

*GEORGE LEE, ornamenter, Chestnut Alley (1819)

RICHARD LEE, chairmaker, corner of Lombard and Eutaw Streets (1837)

CHARLES LEFEVRE, cabinetmaker, N. Sharp Street near Fayette (1833) ; Vine Street east of Pine (1837) ; Orleans Street near Aisquith (1840)

SAMUEL LEGRANT, picture frame maker, Second Street (1800-01)

GOTFRIED LEIBER, piano maker, corner of Pennsylvania Avenue and Biddle Street (1840)

WILLIAM LEONARD, cabinetmaker, 76 Conway Street (1835)

WILLIAM M. LEONARD, cabinetmaker, 2 Perry Street (1837)

————— LESLIE, cabinetmaker, 107 Howard Street south of Conway (1840)

WILLIAM B. LEWIS, cabinetmaker, 27 S. Calvert Street (1837)

WILLOUGHBY LEWIS, cabinetmaker, McElderry Street, o.t. (1812, 1814-15, 1817-18)

HENRY LEYMOURS, cabinetmaker, William Alley near William Street (1835)

JOHN LIGHTBODY, chairmaker, Orleans Street (1833)

ANDREW LIGHTS, cabinetmaker, George Street east of Pine (1837) ; Orchard Street south of Ross (1840)

AUGUSTUS LIHAULT, cabinetmaker, Triplet's Alley near Second Street (1803)

CHARLES LINDENBERGER, cabinetmaker, Whiskey Alley (1804)

HENRY LINGINFELTER, cabinetmaker, Lee Street east of Charles (1837, 1840)

JAMES LITTLE, chairmaker, Potter Street, east side south of Low (1827) ; corner of Fleet and Ann Streets (1829)

HUGH LOGAN, cabinetmaker, 50 N. Liberty Street (1835)

H. M. LOGAN, cabinetmaker, 11 New Church Street (1837, 1840)

JAMES H. LOGAN, cabinetmaker, Franklin Street east of Chattsworth (1840)

CHRISTIAN LOOKY/LUCKY, cabinetmaker, Lerew's Alley (1804) ; Mulberry Alley (1810)

ROBERT LOW, chairmaker, 36 N. Frederick Street (1824)

L. LUDDEN & CO., chairmakers, 8 N. Liberty Street (1827)

LEMUEL LUDDEN, chairmaker, dwelling, Barnett Street, north side east of N. Sharp (1837)

HENRY LUSBY, cabinetmaker, 27 Harrison Street (1817-18) ; 64 High Street, o.t. (1819) ; furniture wareroom, 30 W. Pratt Street (1831)

GEORGE LUTES, cabinetmaker, 3 Painter's Court near Pitt Street (1831)

JOHN S. MACHER, cabinetmaker, German Street west of Cove (1840)

JOHN MAGER, furniture store, 53 Eutaw Street south of Saratoga (1840)

BENJAMIN MAGNESS, chairmaker, corner of Bank and Thames Streets (1835) ; 3 Temple Street (1837) ; Aisquith Street north of Low (1840)

JAMES MANN, cabinetmaker, Stillhouse Street, o.t. (1817-18)

SAMUEL MANSHIP, cabinetmaker, S. Charles Street, west side north of Conway (1827) ; Painter's Court south of Pitt (1829) ; 89 N. Gay Street (1831)

*GALE MARCH, chairmaker, St. Paul's Lane (1812, 1814-15) ; fancy chairmaker, 56 Hanover Street (1816, 1817-18, 1819, 1822-23, 1824)

HENRY MARFIELD, cabinetmaker, Baltimore Street near Paca (1833, 1835)

*MARKLAND & BASSFORD, fancy windsor chair factors, 72 S. Charles Street (1827)

*WILLIAM MARKLAND, firm of Markland & Bassford, dwelling, N. Gay Street, east side north of Green (1827)

EDWARD MARQUAM, cabinetmaker, 17 Water Street (1800-01) ; 55 South Street (1802, 1803)

JAMES MARSH, late looking glass factor, Mulberry Street near Howard (1804)

SIDENHAM MARSH, cabinetmaker, firm of Davenport & Marsh, dwelling, Great York Street, south side west of Harford Run (1824)

C. MARTIN, cabinetmaker, Pine Street near Pierce (1833)

*GEORGE MARTIN, painter, corner of Gay and N. Frederick Streets (1812) ; ornamental painter, Green Street, east side north of Necessity Alley, o.t. (1824) ; 60 S. High Street (1831) ; High Street north of Pratt (1837)

JAMES MARTIN, cabinetmaker, Lovely Lane (1800-01, 1802, 1803, 1804, 1814-15, 1816)

SIMON MARTIN, cabinetmaker, 231 N. Howard Street (1840)

WILLIAM MARTIN, cabinetmaker, 5 Lovely Lane (1807, 1808)

PHILIP MASLIN, cabinetmaker, Potter Street near Gay (1837, 1840)

PHILIP T. MASLIN, cabinetmaker, Orleans Street near the Run (1833)

*AUGUSTUS MATHIOT, chair factory, 42 N. Gay Street, dwelling, Front Street, north side near Low (1827) ; chairmaker, 18 N. Gay Street (1829) ; fancy chair manufactory, 18 N. Gay Street (1831, 1833, 1835) ; chair factory, Gay Street, dwelling, High Street north of Granby (1837, 1840)

A. & J. B. MATHIOT, chair factory, Gay Street near Fayette (1840)

J. B. MATHIOT, corner of Ensor and East Streets (1840)

JOHN MATTHEWS, cabinetmaker, Eutaw Street south of Baltimore (1837)

JOHN MATTHIAS, cabinetmaker, 104 Eutaw Street (1837, 1840)

JAMES MATTIMER, cabinetmaker, Fawn Street, north side near Preston (1827)

HAMMER MATTOX, cabinetmaker, Park Lane west of Pearl Street (1837)

JAMES MAY, chairmaker, Park Street south of Lexington (1837)

JAMES A. MAY, chair manufacturer, 32 Fayette Street near Howard, dwelling, opposite (1840)

JOHN McALLISTER/McCALLISTER, chair manufacturer, 24 Harrison Street, dwelling, Forrest Street near Ensor (1825)

WILLIAM McCARDELL, cabinetmaker, 79 northwest corner of Howard and Saratoga Streets (1827, 1829) ; cabinet and patent bedstead maker, northwest corner of Howard and Saratoga Streets (1831)

JAMES McCLASH, cabinetmaker, Pitt Street east of High, o.t. (1819)

*MATTHEW McCOLM, fancy and windsor chairmaker, 51 South Street (1803, 1804, 1807) ; chairmaker, 45 South Street (1810, 1814-15, 1816, 1817-18) ; fancy and windsor chair factory, 45 South Street (1819) ; chair factory, 45 South Street (1822, 1824, 1827) ; chairmaker, 45 South Street (1829) ; chair factory, 45 South Street (1833, 1835, 1837, 1840)

WALTER A. McCONCHIE, cabinetmaker, Beuren Street (1831)

JAMES McCORMICK, cabinetmaker, Holiday Street, o.t. (1812)

GEORGE McCOUL, cabinetmaker, 33 Liberty Street near Lombard (1829) ; Forrest Street north of Douglass (1831, 1833, 1835) ; furniture wareroom, N. Gay Street near engine house (1837, 1840)

JOHN McCRACKEN, cabinetmaker, 30 S. Charles Street (1824) ; 8 N. Charles Street (1827) ; 49 S. Charles Street (1829, 1831, 1833, 1835, 1837, 1840)

J. & W. McCRACKEN, cabinetmakers, 85 Pratt Street west of Howard (1840)

DAVID McCRAITES/McCREIGHT, cabinetmaker, 76 Conway Street (1837); 103 Howard Street south of Conway (1840)

JOHN McCREADY, carver and gilder, 33 Union Street, o.t. (1810)

CHARLES McDONALD, chairmaker, Conway Street (1833)

*McDONALD and HAYS, house, sign and ornamental painters, southeast corner of Liberty and Conewago Streets (1824)

*JAMES McDONALD, firm of McDonald and Hays, painter, dwelling, 88 North Street (1824)

SAMUEL McELROY, cabinetmaker, Prince Street, o.t. (1817-18); William's Alley, south side east of Spring Street (1822-23, 1824)

JOHN McELWEE, looking glass, oil and color store, 2 S. Calvert Street (1804); gilder, 2 S. Calvert Street (1808)

*JAMES McGIBBON, painter and gilder, 42 N. Gay Street, dwelling, 65 Harrison Street (1819)

*JOHN McGOLDRICK, carver and gilder, 51 N. Gay Street, dwelling, 60 N. Frederick (1819)

JOHN N. McJILTON, cabinetmaker, 11 Sharp Street, dwelling, Rock Street between Saratoga and Lexington (1829)

FRANCIS T. McKINLEY, cabinetmaker, Constitution Street near French (1840)

ADAMS L. McLEANS, furniture store, 17 W. Water Street (1831)

PAUL McSWEENEY, cabinetmaker, Richmond near Tyson (1819)

MICHAEL MEAD, cabinetmaker, E. Baltimore Street, north side between Spring and Caroline (1827)

NICHOLAS MEAD, cabinetmaker, Ensor Street near East (1829); Baltimore Street east of Eden (1831); Eden Street south of Orleans (1835)

ELIJAH MEDCALF, cabinetmaker, Eutaw Street, west side north of Lombard (1824); northwest corner of Aisquith Street and Straight Lane (1827); 3 Mercer Street west of Calvert (1829); Maiden Lane (1833); Pitt Street west of Harford Run (1835); 97 Eutaw Street 4 doors north of Camden (1840)

JAMES MERRIKEN, cabinetmaker, N. Eutaw Street (1810); 8 Lexington Street (1814-15); 16 N. Frederick Street (1817-18); Lerew's Alley near Saratoga Street (1819); cabinetmaker and sexton of St. Paul's Episcopal Church, dwelling, 10 Lexington Street (1822-23, 1824, 1827, 1829); cabinetmaker, 8 Lexington Street (1831, 1833, 1835)

DIERK MEYER, chairmaker, corner of Wilk and Exeter Streets (1840)

JOHN MEYER, cabinetmaker, German Street east of Howard (1840)

*JOHN MICHAU, carver, gilder and picture frame maker, southwest corner of Commerce and Water Streets (1824)

HENRY MILLER, cabinetmaker, Sharp Street near Hill (1837, 1840)

JAMES MILLER, chairmaker, 42 South Street (1835)

JOHN MILLER, chairmaker, 52 Wilks Street, f.p. (1800-01)

MR. MINSEY, cabinetmaker, French Street north of Front (1835)

1

SAMUEL MINSKEY, cabinetmaker, 61 St. Patrick's Row, dwelling, Prince Street near Albemarle (1810); cabinet warehouses, 54 and 61 St. Patrick's Row (1812)

WILLIAM MITCHELL, chairmaker, E. Pratt Street near the bridge (1817-18); 42 Fayette Street (1819); North Street south of Lexington (1819); chair factory, 21 Pratt Street (1822-23, 1824); chairmaker, 13 Sharp Street, dwelling, Conway near Eutaw (1829)

WILLIAM H. MOBLEY, cabinetmaker, W. Baltimore Street near Eutaw (1833)

MARMADUKE MOLLE, cabinetmaker, Bridge Street near Front, o.t. (1819)

MOLLEE & SECHE, cabinetmakers, 8 Bridge Street, o.t. (1817-18)

*J. MONSARRAT, ornamental painter and japanner, 5 Conewago Street (1819)

JAMES MOORE, cabinetmaker, Bond Street near Gough, f.p. (1817-18)

JAMES A. MOORE, cabinetmaker, Forrest Street south of Douglass (1835, 1840)

JAMES MORRISON, cabinetmaker, Vine Street (1819); chairmaker, East Street, west side north of Hill (1827); Ensor Street near Mott (1833)

JAMES MORTIMER, cabinetmaker, Bishop's Alley, corner of Little York, o.t. (1824); 9 Fish Market Space (1833); Bond Street north of Gough (1840)

JOHN MORTON, cabinetmaker, 29 Pratt Street, dwelling, Duke Street (1807); 29 Bond Street, f.p. (1808, 1810); dwelling, Duke Street near Wolfe, o.t. (1810); 98 Bond Street, f.p. (1814-15); 102 Bond Street, f.p. (1816, 1817-18); southeast corner of Bond and Fleet Streets, f.p. (1822-23, 1824)

HENRY MOST, cabinetmaker, 16 Center Market Space (1827); 61 Center Market Space (1829)

JOHN M. MUHLHOFER, cabinetmaker, 81 Harrison Street (1833); Saratoga Street east of Holliday (1837, 1840)

WILLIAM H. MULLIKIN, cabinetmaker, Forrest Street north of Ensor (1829); 8 Mulberry Street (1831); 43 N. Gay Street (1833)

RICHARD MUNROE, cabinetmaker, 33 Harrison Street (1817-18)

JOHN MURRAY, chairmaker, Fayette Street east of Howard (1840)

WILLIAM MURRAY, cabinetmaker, 98 Sharp Street (1833); Lexington Street near Liberty (1835, 1837, 1840)

RICHMOND MURROE, cabinetmaker, 70 Cumberland Row (1816)

HENRY MYERS, cabinetmaker, 61 Center Market Space (1840)

J. D. MYERS, cabinetmaker, 10 Peace Alley (1833)

JAMES NEAL, cabinetmaker, Elbow Lane (1833)

E. NEEDLES & CO., 56 Hanover Street (1831)

EDWARD NEEDLES, chairmaker, 56 Hanover Street, dwelling, Hanover Street opposite Sharp (1827); 55 Hanover Street (1829); 56 Hanover Street (1831, 1833)

JOHN NEEDLES, cabinet manufacturer, opposite Indian Queen Hotel, Hanover Street, dwelling, 5 German Lane (1812); cabinetmaker, 8 Hanover Street, dwelling, 54 Hanover Street (1814-15, 1816, 1817-18, 1819, 1822-23, 1824, 1827); manufacturer of cabinet furniture, 54 Hanover Street, dwelling, 55 Hanover Street (1829, 1831); cabinetmaker and upholsterer, 54 Hanover Street, dwelling, 53 Hanover Street (1835); cabinetmaker and dry goods merchant, 54 Hanover Street, dwelling, 47 Hanover Street (1837, 1840)

JOHN NEFF, cabinetmaker, 53 Hanover Street (1831)

PETER NEUVELLE, cabinetmaker, Saratoga Street near Charles (1814-15)

CHARLES NEWBALL, cabinetmaker, Wolf Street west of Caroline (1837)

m

JACOB NEWCOMMER, chairmaker, 39 Charles Street (1800-01) ; 20 Pratt Street (1802, 1803)

SAMUEL NEWTON, cabinetmaker, over 63 Center Market Space (1827)

THOMAS NICHOLSON, cabinetmaker, Baltimore Street north side west of Washington Lane (1822-23)

ROBERT H. NORRIS, cabinetmaker, 93 W. Pratt Street (1819, 1822-23, 1824)

JAMES NORTHWOOD, cabinetmaker, Hanover Street south of Sugar Alley (1837)

PETER NOUVELLE, cabinetmaker, S. Charles Street east of Pratt (1833)

DAVID OGDEN, cabinetmaker, dwelling, Pleasant Street near the corner of Holliday Street (1812) ; Orange Alley (1814-15)

JONATHAN OGDEN, cabinetmaker, dwelling, Concord Street (1812) ; dwelling, 6 Conewago Street (1814-15) ; dwelling, Vulcan Alley (1816, 1822-23) ; 10 New Church Street (1831)

OGDEN & CALDWELL'S CABINET MANU-FACTORY, 11 South Street (1812, 1814-15)

JAMES OGLE, chairmaker, 72½ Green Street (1822-23) ; cane chair bottomer, Harford Avenue west of Aisquith, o.t. (1824) ; Liberty Alley, west side near the jail (1827)

WILLIAM OGLE, windsor chairmaker, Duke Street near Albemarle and Granby (1804) ; chairmaker, Mott Street near Sterling (1833)

JACOB OLDHAM, chairmaker, Whiskey Alley (1802, 1803, 1804) ; Pratt Street near Howard (1810) ; 94 Pratt Street (1814-15, 1816, 1817-18, 1819) ; 72 S. Charles Street (1824) ; 42 W. Pratt Street (1827) ; 9 Mercer Street (1831) ; Charles Street (1833)

JOHN OLDHAM, chairmaker, dwelling, 43 South Street, shop between 66 and 68 South Street (1800-01) ; chair manufacturer, 70 South Street (1802, 1803) also, dwelling, next 94 Pratt Street (1803) : chairmaker, near 67 South Street (1804) ; dwelling, 92 Pratt Street, shop, 68 South Street (1807, 1808) ; dwelling, 40 South Street, shop, 74 South Street (1810, 1814-15) ; 70 South Street, dwelling, 40 South Street (1816, 1817-18, 1819, 1822-23, 1824, 1827, 1829, 1831, 1833, 1835)

THOMAS OLDHAM, chairmaker, Barre Street (1810) ; 70 Pratt Street near Commerce, dwelling, 76 Camden Street (1812)

*LAWRENCE O'LONGLAN, ornamental painter, Harford Avenue north of Herber's rope walk (1824)

THOMAS OPPERMAN, chairmaker, Wolf's Alley between Peace Alley and Conway Street (1831)

JOSEPH ORSBOURN, cabinetmaker, 15 Harrison Street (1819)

CHRISTIAN OSTERMAN, cabinetmaker, Thames Street east of Bond (1840)

JAMES OTLEY, windsor chairmaker, 16 Union Street (1803)

THOMAS H. OWENS, Eager Alley north of Saratoga Street (1837)

*THOMAS PALMER, carver and gilder, Conewago Street, south side east of Liberty (1824)

GOTTLIEB PARDOLOME, cabinetmaker, Pratt Street east of the bridge (1840)

CHARLES PARKER, cabinetmaker, Canal Street fronting Pratt (1840)

SILAS PARKER, cabinetmaker, 30 N. Frederick Street (1817-18)

JOHN PARKS, cabinetmaker, 6 Peace Alley (1833)

JOHN PARR, cabinetmaker, 48 Front Street, shop in Second Street (1803, 1804) ; 23 Second Street (1807, 1808, 1810)

STEPHEN PARRISH, cabinetmaker, Union Street, east side south of French, o.t. (1824) ; Rock Street near Saratoga (1833) ; Union Street east of Pennsylvania Avenue (1835)

SAMUEL PASSMORE, cabinetmaker, 7 Saratoga Street (1810)

GEORGE PATTON, cabinetmaker, 1 door from the corner of Pratt and Mulberry Streets (1833) ; Saratoga Street west of Chattsworth (1837)

JAMES H. PATTON, cabinetmaker, Brandy Alley near Eutaw Street (1819) ; 23½ S. Calvert Street, dwelling, Waterloo Alley (1822-23) ; 23 S. Calvert Street, dwelling, Lovely Lane (1824) ; Water Street, north side east of South (1827) ; Camden Street near Market (1831) ; 110 Sharp Street (1833, 1835, 1837) ; 31 Hanover Street north of Lombard, dwelling, Sharp Street 1 door south of Barre (1840)

WILLIAM PATTERSON, cabinetmaker, 22 Albemarle Street (1802, 1803, 1804, 1807, 1808, 1810, 1814-15, 1816, 1817-18)

SAMUEL D. PAYNE, cabinetmaker, Pennsylvania Avenue, north side west of Montgomery (1824)

INGRAM E. PEACOCK, umbrella and chairmaker, Pratt Street east of Howard (1840)

LAONPECOR PECOR, cabinetmaker, 69 Harrison Street (1829)

ALFRED PEIRCE, furnishing store, 249 W. Baltimore Street (1840)

*JAMES PENNINGTON, fancy chairmaker, Short Street (1819) ; chairmaker, west side east of Jefferson (1822-23) ; Low Street west of Aisquith (1829) ; Aisquith Street between Orleans and Jefferson (1831, 1833) ; Harford Road north of the lumber yard (1835) ; 7 Bank Lane (1837) ; Aisquith Street near Thompson (1840)

CONRAD PEOPET, cabinetmaker, Pennsylvania Avenue south of Hoffman Street (1835)

THOMAS R. PERKINS, cabinetmaker, 98 W. Pratt Street (1833)

JOHN C. PETHERBRIDGE, cabinetmaker, 2 Granby Street, o.t. (1812)

WALTER PHELPS, cabinetmaker, Pine Street south of George (1835)

BENJAMIN PHILLIPS, windsor chairmaker, corner of Bond and Aliceanna Streets, f.p. (1803)

JAMES PHILIPS, cabinetmaker, Front Street north of Baltimore (1829)

*RICHARD PHILIPS, painter and gilder, 26 South Street (1807, 1808) ; sign painter and ornamental gilder, 9 Calvert Street (1816) ; sign painter and gilder on glass, 5 Bank Street, dwelling, Water Street west of Calvert (1819) ; sign painter and gilder on glass, 127 N. Eutaw Street (1829)

WILLIAM PHILLIPS, cabinetmaker, 78 Petticoat Alley, f.p. (1810) ; corner of Cove Street and Pennsylvania Avenue (1819, 1822-23, 1824) ; 46 Front Street (1827) ; Pitt Street (1831, 1833) ; 23 Sterling Street (1837, 1840)

LACHLAN PHYF, cabinetmaker, 37 S. Gay Street (1807, 1808)

GEORGE PLANE, cabinetmaker, 14 Green Street (1816, 1817-18, 1819)

WILLIAM T. PLUMMER, cabinetmaker, 5 Water Street (1831)

THOMAS POE, cabinetmaker, S. Frederick Street (1803) ; King George Street (1804) ; Aisquith Street (1810, 1814-15, 1816, 1817-18) ; Duke Street, south side west of Albemarle (1822-23, 1824)

*SETH POLLARD, ornamental painter, 13 Potter Street (1816, 1817-18) ; Apple Alley near Smith Street (1819)

EBENEZER POOL, cabinetmaker, Commerce Street (1831)

LEWIS POPE, cabinet and chairmaker, Pennsylvania Avenue south of Hoffman Street (1835)

RANDOLPH POPE, cabinetmaker, Canal Street north of Jefferson (1840)

C. POUILIHAN, cabinetmaker, 35 S. Gay Street (1807, 1808)

DANIEL POWLES, cabinet and chairmaker, northwest corner of Howard and Saratoga Streets (1822-23, 1824) ; cabinetmaker, Pearl Street, west side south of Lexington (1827)

HENRY POWLES, cabinetmaker, Pine Street near Franklin (1831) ; cabinet and chairmaker, corner of Howard and Saratoga Streets (1835, 1837, 1840)

JOHN POYTREE, cabinetmaker, Constitution Street, east side near the jail (1827)

HENRY PRATT, cabinetmaker, Baltimore Street 2 doors west of Cove (1840)

HENRY PRESTON, cabinetmaker, Mulberry Street west of Pearl (1837, 1840)

PRICE & PARR, cabinetmakers, Second Street near Frederick and Gay (1804)

R. PRICE, cabinetmaker, dwelling, Triplet's Alley (1804)

WARWICK PRICE, cabinetmaker, 136 High Street, o.t. (1800-01) ; 45 Bridge Street, dwelling, 136 High Street (1802, 1803, 1804, 1807, 1808, 1810)

EDWARD PRIESTLEY, cabinetmaker, 2 Baltimore Street (1808) ; next 4 Baltimore Street, dwelling, 12 Harrison Street (1810, 1814-15) ; Market Street near the Bridge (1816) ; 4 Baltimore Street (1817-18) ; 4 Baltimore Street, dwelling, 12 Harrison Street (1819, 1822-23, 1824) ; dwelling, 2 Albemarle Street (1829) ; 6 Baltimore Street, dwelling, Front Street north of Pitt (1831, 1833) ; 4 Baltimore Street (1835)

PRIESTLEY & MINSKEY, cabinetmakers, 79 Water Street (1802, 1803, 1804) ; 6 Baltimore Street (1807, 1808)

PRIMROSE & RUSSELL, carpenters and cabinetmakers, Saratoga Street west of Gay (1829, 1831) ; 19 N. Gay Street (1835)

LEMUEL S. PRINCE, cabinetmaker, Potter Street north of Low (1829, 1831)

LEVIN PRITCHARD, cabinetmaker, East Street near Pitt (1833, 1835, 1837, 1840)

THOMAS PRITCHARD, cabinetmaker, 54 Happy Alley (1829, 1831)

LEVIN PRITCHEL, cabinetmaker, Liberty Street, west side north of Pitt (1822-23)

ELIJAH PRITCHETT, cabinetmaker, 5 Comet Street, o.t. (1817-18, 1819)

HENRY PURCELL, cabinetmaker, 66 South Street (1800-01)

MATTHEW PURDEN, chairmaker, Salisbury Street west of Exeter (1835)

WILLIAM PURDY, cabinetmaker, W. Pratt Street near Eutaw (1833)

PHILIP RAAB, piano forte maker, corner of Saratoga and Liberty Streets (1814-15, 1822-23, 1824)

JACOB READ, cabinetmaker, Caroline Street south of Wilk (1835)

JOHN READ/REED/REID, cabinetmaker, 15 Baltimore Street extended (1810, 1814-15, 1816, 1817-18, 1819) ; Baltimore Street, south side near Pearl (1824, 1827) ; 109 N. Eutaw Street (1835)

——— REINHART, cabinetmaker, Saratoga Street opposite African Church (1840)

ROBERT REINWICK, cabinetmaker, Hill Street near Light (1837)

FRANCIS RENAULT, cabinetmaker, Caroline Street near Wilk, f.p. (1817-18)

ROBERT RENNICK, cabinetmaker, corner of Forrest Street and Harford Run (1840)

THOMAS S. RENSHAW, cabinetmaker, 37 S. Gay Street (1814-15)

SAMUEL RETAN/RATAN, cabinetmaker, Granby Street west of the Run (1835) ; Eden Street north of Baltimore (1840)

HENRY REUSCH, cabinetmaker, Biddle Street near Ross (1831)

GEORGE RHINEHART, cabinetmaker, Water Street between Gay and Frederick (1837)

JAMES RICHER, chairmaker, Wilk Street near the bridge (1819)

LOVERING RICKETTS, cabinetmaker, 68 French Street, o.t. (1814-15, 1816, 1817-18) ; Bond Street, west side south of Smith (1822-23) ; piano forte maker, Lovely Lane, south side west of South Street (1824) ; 51 Center Market Space (1827)

P

PHILIP RICKETTS, cabinetmaker, Wilk Street east of Bond (1840)

CHARLES RIDDELL, chairmaker, Chamberlain's Alley (1810)

FREDERICK RIDERMAN, cabinetmaker, Green Street south of Baltimore (1837)

NICHOLAS RIDGELY, chairmaker, factory, 53 South Street, dwelling, Lee Street (1840)

ALEXANDER RIGBY, chairmaker, corner of Bond and Wilk Streets, f.p. (1802) ; windsor chairmaker, near 17 Wilk Street (1803) ; chairmaker, W. Wilk Street (1804)

BENJAMIN RINGGOLD, cabinetmaker, 23 Fayette Street (1817-18)

HENRY RIPHA, cabinetmaker, corner of Wilk and Exeter Streets (1840)

SAMUEL J. RITUN, cabinetmaker, 12 Pitt Street (1835)

FRANCIS ROACH, cabinetmaker, Market Street, west side north of Aliceanna (1824)

ABRAHAM ROBINSON, chairmaker, Biddle Street (1812, 1817-18, 1819) ; northwest corner of Park Lane and Green Street (1822-23) ; Baltimore Street east of Booth's Nursery (1827, 1829, 1831, 1833, 1835, 1837) ; Cove Street north of Vine (1840)

*JOHN ROBINSON, chairmaker, 3 Second Street (1812, 1814-15) ; 46 South Street (1816, 1817-18) ; fancy chairmaker, 51 South Street (1819, 1824, 1827, 1831, 1833, 1835, 1837, 1840) ; 51 North Street, dwelling, King George Street, north side east of Exeter (1822-23)

GEORGE C. RODENMAYER, cabinetmaker, Forrest and Ensor Streets (1837, 1840)

DANIEL RODGERS, cabinetmaker, northwest of S. Charles and Conway Streets (1827)

DAVID RODGERS, cabinetmaker, 25 Shakespeare Street, f.p. (1817-18)

A. & G. ROGERS, cabinetmakers, S. Charles Street, east side south of Ruxton Lane (1822-23) ; Charles Street, west side south of Conway, and Charles Street, east side north of Pratt (1824) ; 11 Sharp Street (1827)

ALEXANDER ROGERS, cabinetmaker, 43 Water Street (1817-18) ; Uhler's Alley, dwelling, Hanover Street (1822-23, 1824, 1827)

JOHN ROGERS, cabinetmaker, Duke Street near Harford Run, o.t. (1817-18) ; S. Frederick Street near Baltimore (1819) ; northeast corner of German and Eutaw Streets, dwelling, 27 German Street (1822-23) ; northeast corner of Franklin Street and Lerew's Alley (1824) ; chair factory, 51 South Street (1827)

J. ROGERS, cabinetmaker, Tripolet's Alley south of Baltimore Street (1829)

*ROBERT ROSS, ornamental painter, N. Gay Street near Aisquith (1837) ; Sterling Street near Methodist Church (1840)

ROBERT R. ROSS, chairmaker, corner of German Lane and Sharp Street, dwelling, corner of Lombard and Grant Streets (1831)

WILLIAM B. ROSS, cabinetmaker, Gillingham's Alley (1819) ; 75 W. Pratt Street (1824) ; 58 S. Charles Street (1827, 1829) ; 8 Hanover Street, dwelling, 54 S. Charles Street (1831) ; furniture room, Hanover Street near German Lane (1833)

STEPHEN C. ROSZELL, cabinetmaker, 45 Fayette Street (1835)

LEWIS ROUSTER, cabinetmaker, 91 Bond Street, f.p. (1817-18) ; 24 Fell Street, f.p. (1819) ; 3 Ann Street (1829)

JOHN ROY, cabinetmaker, Mott Street (1831) ; 4 Potter Street (1833)

LOUIS RUECKART, cabinetmaker, 99 Bond Street (1837, 1840)

*CHARLES RUSSELL, ornamental painter, Aisquith Street, east side south of Holland, o.t. (1824)

JACOB RUTH, cabinetmaker, Caroline Street south of Wilk (1840)

SANFORD & CO., furniture store, 36 Light Street (1840)

NICHOLAS SANK, furniture store, Eutaw Street north of Saratoga (1831)

JAMES SANKEY, cabinetmaker, Monument Street east of Eden (1840)

JOHN SARVER, cabinetmaker, Union Street, west side north of Bridge, o.t. (1824)

CHARLES SAUDER, cabinetmaker, Market Street below Thames (1831)

CHARLES SCHDERZER, cabinetmaker, 18 Saratoga Street near Gay (1840)

CHRISTOPHER SCHELER/SCHERER, cabinetmaker, 81 N. Gay Street (1835); 64 Harrison Street (1837, 1840)

WILLIAM SCHERER, cabinetmaker, Armistead Lane east of William Street (1837)

PHILIP SCHMOLFIN, cabinetmaker, 16 Mercer Street (1833)

BALTZELL SCHROEDER, cabinetmaker, 61 Bond Street (1837, 1840)

HARMAN SCHULENBERG, cabinetmaker, Eutaw Street 1 door south of Columbia (1840)

WILLIAM SCHUTTA, cabinetmaker, 18 Saratoga Street near Gay (1840)

MATTHEW SCOTT, cabinetmaker, 6 Shakespeare Street, f.p. (1807, 1808)

SECHE AND HOLLAND, cabinetmakers, Lexington Street west of Fayette (1837)

q

JOSEPH SECHE, cabinetmaker, 36 N. Gay Street (1819); 34 New Church Street (1827); Sharp Street south of Lexington (1829); Park Street south of Lexington (1833, 1835)

FRANCIS SEGON, cabinetmaker, Short Street, o.t. (1819)

*JOHN B. SEIDENSTRICKER, ornamental painter, corner of Tripolett's Alley and Baltimore Street, dwelling, Forrest Street near Hillen (1837); corner of Gay and Exeter Streets (1840)

HENRY SELLEK, cabinetmaker, 33 Union Street (1835)

WILLIAM SELLER, cabinetmaker, 81 Ann Street, f.p. (1800-01); next 58 Bank Street, f.p. (1802); near 148 Bond Street, near Bank (1804); 150 corner of Bank Street, f.p. (1810)

BENJAMIN SEVERSON, cabinetmaker, 35 Water Street (1827, 1829)

THOMAS SEWELL, chairmaker, Peace Alley west of Charles Street (1829); Lee Street between Charles and Hanover, shop, corner of Sharp Street and German Lane (1831); Perry Street east of Charles (1837)

WILLIAM SHAMBERG, chairmaker, Cider Alley west of Paca Street (1831, 1833)

WILLIAM SHANNON, furniture rooms, Gay Street near Potter (1837, 1840)

SAMUEL SHARKE, cabinetmaker, 16 Commerce Street (1829)

THOMAS SHERWOOD, cabinet and chairmaker, 127 Bond Street, f.p. (1802, 1803, 1804)

HARMAN SHILLINGBERG, cabinetmaker, Lee Street east of Charles (1837)

SAMUEL SHOCK, cabinetmaker, Commerce Street (1827); 28 E. Water Street (1829, 1833, 1835)

MORRIS A. SHOEMAKER/SCHUMACHER, cabinetmaker, 48 S. Charles Street (1824); Sarah Ann Street east of Cove (1829, 1835)

JOHN SHOWAKER, cabinetmaker, Park Street, west side north of Fayette (1827)

HENRY S. SHRYOCK, cabinetmaker, 32 New Church Street (1835, 1837) ; 24 New Church Street (1840)

AUGUSTUS P. SHUTT, chair wareroom, 36 Lombard Street east of Frederick (1840)

WILLIAM SIGLER, chairmaker, 48 Harrison Street (1840)

CHARLES P. SIMONSON, chairmaker, Lombard Street near Light (1835, 1837) ; 299 Baltimore Street west of Paca (1840)

JOHN SIMONSON, chairmaker, 58 Light Street (1812) ; cabinetmaker, 58 Light Street (1814-15) ; chairmaker, 59 Light Street (1816, 1817-18, 1819, 1822-23, 1824, 1827, 1829, 1831, 1833) ; 11 W. Pratt Street (1835) ; 55 Hanover Street (1837, 1840)

ANDREW SIMMONS, cabinetmaker, East Street near Bridge, o.t. (1810)

HENRY SIMMONS, cabinetmaker, 16 Fayette Street (1804) ; 74 Front Street, o.t. (1807, 1808)

WILLIAM SIMPSON, cabinetmaker, Falls Street (1831)

HENRY SINGER, cabinetmaker, Holland Street west of Harford Run (1835)

WILLIAM SINGLETON, cabinetmaker, dwelling, 11 N. Gay Street (1800-01, 1802, 1803)

ROBERT SKILLMAN, chairmaker, 60 Cumberland Row (1810) ; 32 Hanover Street (1835) ; 36 S. High Street (1837) ; Maiden Lane (1840)

SKILLMAN & SWAIN, chair factors, 49 South Street, Jacob Skillman, dwelling, Exeter Street (1824)

EDWARD SMITH, chairmaker, 17 Harrison Street (1833)

FREDERICK SMITH, cabinetmaker, corner of Hanover Street and Busy Alley (1819, 1822-23) ; northeast corner of Pratt and Commerce Streets (1824)

r

*GEORGE SMITH, carver and gilder, Great York Street, o.t. (1800-01, 1803, 1804) ; 174 Baltimore Street (1808) ; 154 Baltimore Street (1810) ; 174 Baltimore Street (1812) ; 3 Great York Street, o.t. (1814-15) ; opposite Christ Church, Front Street, o.t. (1816) ; 5 S. Gay Street (1819) ; cabinetmaker, Howard Street 1 door north of Clay, dwelling, Marion Street east of Howard (1840)

JOSEPH F. SMITH, cabinetmaker, 24 New Church Street (1837) ; Cove Street south of Mulberry (1840)

RINGGOLD SMITH, chair factory, 49 South Street (1833, 1835, 1837, 1840)

RINGOLD SMITH, chairmaker, 89 Exeter Street (1837)

THOMAS SMITH, cabinetmaker, 17 Water Street west of Center Market Space (1827, 1829) ; 5 Commerce Street (1831) ; 3 Commerce Street (1833) ; 5 Commerce Street (1835, 1837, 1840) and also, furniture store, Eutaw Street north of Lexington (1840)

WILLIAM SNUGGRASS, chairmaker, 16 N. Frederick Street (1800-01) ; windsor chairmaker, Hook's Town turryside road (1803)

JOHN SORAN, chairmaker, Maiden Lane near Aisquith Street (1829) ; corner of Bond and Gough Streets (1833, 1835, 1837, 1840)

JOHN SOUTHERLAND/SUTHERLAND, cabinetmaker, Strawberry Alley north of German Street (1817-18) ; north end of Happy Alley, f.p. (1819) ; Wolf Street, east side south of Wilk (1822-23) ; Happy Alley (1824)

CHARLES SPRINKLEY, chairmaker, Caroline Street south of Orleans (1840)

JONATHAN SPRY, cabinetmaker, Montgomery Street west of Light (1831)

*U. B. STAMMEN, ornamental painter, 13 Comet Street, o.t. (1819, 1833, 1835, 1837, 1840)

*JOHN STAPLES, fancy chairmaker, corner of North and Forrest Streets, o.t. (1810)

DAVID STAPLETON, cabinetmaker, Eutaw Street north of Saratoga (1835) ; corner of Pratt and Sharp Streets (1840)

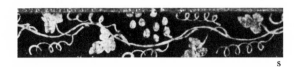

L. S. STARR, cabinetmaker, Light Street (1807, 1808)

DAVID STEEL, cabinetmaker, Peace Alley near Eutaw Street (1833) ; 7 Commerce Street (1835) ; 107 S. Howard Street (1837) ; Park Street 2 doors south of Lexington (1840)

THOMAS STERLING, chairmaker, 72 Pitt Street (1822-23)

TIMOTHY STEVENS, cabinetmaker, 98 Bond Street, f.p. (1819)

J. STEVENSON, cabinetmaker, 7 High Street, o.t. (1807, 1808, 1810)

ROBERT STEVENSON, chairmaker, 50 S. Frederick Street (1840)

ADAM STEWART, piano forte manufacture, 8 N. Charles Street (1812)

JAMES STEWART, piano forte maker, St. Paul's Lane (1814-15, 1816) ; 96 Hanover Street, corner of Conway (1817-18)

THOMAS STEWART, piano forte maker, 175 Hanover Street (1819)

STICHER & CLEMENS, cabinetmaker, 41 South Street (1804)

JOHN STICHER/STITCHER, cabinetmaker, 33 South Street (1803) ; Camden Street (1804) ; Park Street, west side south of Franklin (1827, 1829, 1833, 1835, 1837)

PETER STICHER/STITCHER, cabinetmaker, 41 Fayette Street (1810)

MEGILE STIENER, cabinetmaker, Franklin Street east of Paca (1835)

HENRY STITZENBERG, cabinetmaker, Light Street near Lee (1840)

STORK & FREELAND, cabinetmakers, 43 Franklin Street (1833)

JOHN STORK, cabinetmaker, 109 Green Street (1837)

RICHARD STORK, chairmaker, Monument Street 2 doors east of Ensor (1840)

JAMES STORM, chairmaker, 104 Exeter Street north of Gay (1829) ; Pennsylvania Avenue near Franklin Street (1831, 1833)

JOSEPH STOUT, cabinetmaker, Potter Street, east side south of Low (1827, 1829)

F. STRINGER, cabinetmaker, N. Liberty Street near Lexington (1804)

HENRY STUFFELMAN, cabinetmaker, 31 Union Street (1817-18) ; 33 Union Street (1824)

CHRISTIAN STURN, piano manufacturer, Liberty Street 1 door south of German (1840)

WILLIAM SURRELL, cabinetmaker, 103 N. Howard Street (1819)

CHARLES SUTER, cabinetmaker, 59 Albemarle Street (1833) ; Pratt Street near bridge, dwelling, President Street near Pratt (1837, 1840)

HENRY SUTER, cabinetmaker, Carolina Street near Gough, f.p. (1819)

STEPHEN SWAIN, chair factor, 49 South Street (1829)

JOHN SWAN, chairmaker, 51 E. Baltimore Street (1831)

DENNIS SWEANY, chairmaker, 142 N. High Street (1829)

PAUL SWEENY/SWEENEY, cabinetmaker, Forrest Lane (1803) ; 16 Fayette Street (1803, 1804, 1814-15) ; 82 Camden Street (1816)

RICHARD SWEENY/SWEENEY, windsor chairmaker, shop, adjoining Baltimore Street bridge, dwelling, 61 Front Street (1800-01, 1802, 1803, 1804) ; chairmaker, corner of Bond and Wilk Streets (1810) ; Harford Street, o.t. (1812) ; 23 Carolina Street, dwelling, corner of Exeter and Wilk Streets, o.t. (1819) ; Wilk Street, west end, dwelling, corner of Bank and Eden Streets (1827, 1829, 1831) ; 48 S. High Street (1833) ; 33 High Street (1835, 1837)

Thos RENSHAW Nº 37 S. Gay St Baltᵉ

———— TARR, cabinetmaker, Orleans Street 2 doors east of Friendship (1835)

EDWIN S. TARR, cabinet and venetian blind maker, 37 Harrison Street (1819); 3 North Street, dwelling, Gay Street extended near Mott (1829); cabinetmaker, wareroom, 4 North Street near Baltimore, dwelling, N. Gay Street (1831); 28 North Street (1833); 41 N. Gay Street (1835, 1840)

LEVIN S. TARR, cabinetmaker, shop, 28 Light Street, dwelling, Dutch Alley (1802, 1803, 1804, 1814-15)

TARR & SHERWOOD, cabinetmakers, back of 65 Baltimore Street and back of 45 South Street (1800-01)

WESLEY B. TARR, cabinetmaker, 32 Gay Street, dwelling, Front Street 4th door south of Low (1840)

WILLIAM TARR, cabinetmaker, N. Gay Street near Mott (1837, 1840)

JOHN B. TAYLOR, cabinetmaker, 32 N. Gay Street (1810); 32 Water Street (1812)

DANIEL TEVIS, cabinetmaker, 10 Fayette Street (1822-23); 16 Fayette Street (1824, 1827, 1829, 1831, 1833)

JAMES THOMAS, cabinetmaker, corner of Exeter and Hillen Streets (1835); Low Street north of Exeter (1837)

JOSEPH THOMAS, cabinetmaker, 128 High Street (1835)

JOSEPH P. THOMAS, cabinetmaker, corner of Mott and Sterling Streets (1833)

LAMBERT THOMAS, cabinetmaker, Low Street near High, o.t. (1810); 35 Bridge Street, o.t. (1812, 1814-15, 1816); 132 High Street (1817-18); corner of Bridge and High Streets, o.t. (1819); 128 High Street, o.t. (1822-23, 1824, 1827, 1831, 1833)

STERLING THOMAS, chairmaker, Aisquith Street (1814-15); 17 Comet Street, o.t. (1816); 41 Green Street, o.t. (1817-18, 1819)

SAMUEL THOMPSON, cabinetmaker, Harrison Street, west side near Baltimore, dwelling, Holliday Street, west side south of Pleasant (1824); dwelling, N. Calvert Street near City Spring (1827); 13 Harrison Street (1829, 1831, 1833, 1837, 1840)

THOMAS JEFFERSON THOMPSON, chairmaker, Franklin Row 4th house west of Chattsworth Street (1831, 1833); French Street 2 doors east of Potter (1840)

WILLIAM THOMPSON, cabinetmaker, Lexington Street (1800-01, 1802, 1803)

EDWARD THURSTON, japanner, Mercer Street near Light (1835)

*PHILIP AND WILLIAM TILYARD, sign and ornamental painters, 6 N. Charles Street, dwelling, 3 Saratoga Street (1812)

SAMUEL TITUS, cabinetmaker, 86 Harrison Street (1817-18)

CONRAD TOBER, cabinetmaker, Jackson Street east of Aisquith (1840)

DAVID TOOL/TOOLE, chairmaker, 2 Potter Street (1829, 1831); Forrest Street (1833); Jackson Street, south side (1835); Forrest Street west of Harford Run (1837)

FREDERICK TORSCH, cabinetmaker, Short Alley near Conway Street (1833)

FREDERICK TOSH, cabinetmaker, York Street near Charles (1835)

*BENNETT TOWMAN, ornamental painter, 13 Comet Street, o.t. (1824)

DAVID TOWNSEND, chairmaker, 39 Franklin Street west of Eutaw (1831)

MATHIAS B. TOWNSEND, cabinetmaker, 12 N. Gay Street (1829); 44 Second Street (1831)

HENRY TREBE, cabinetmaker, 58 N. Exeter Street (1837)

DAVID TUCKER, chairmaker, Caroline Street, f.p. (1800-01)

GEORGE H. TUCKER, carpenter and cabinetmaker, 255 N. Gay Street (1831); cabinetmaker, 9 Second Street (1835)

JOHN H. TUCKER, chairmaker, Pratt Street, north side near Exeter (1831, 1833, 1835, 1837); Exchange Place, dwelling, Exeter Street 1 door south of Fawn (1840)

TUCKER & ROBINSON, chair factory, 5 Exchange Place (1840)

NATHANIEL UNAM, cabinetmaker, 46 S. Charles Street (1817-18)

THOMAS UPPERMAN, chairmaker, Sugar Alley (1833)

JAMES VAN BUREN/VAN BEUREN, piano forte maker, 19 Saratoga Street (1812); corner of Bath and Holliday Streets (1816)

RICHARD W. VARDEN, chairmaker, Eden Street south of Gough (1837)

JOHN VARNISH, cabinetmaker, Britton Street southwest of Neighbour (1835)

JESSE VICKERS, chairmaker, Petticoat Alley, f.p. (1817-18); Harford Avenue, east side south of Gough (1822-23); Eden Street, west side south of German, f.p. (1824); Gough Street, south side (1827, 1829); Crook's back row, Monument Street (1831); Falls Street near Beuren (1833); Eden Street 4 doors from Holland (1840)

JOHN N. VINCENT, cabinetmaker, Orleans Street west of Aisquith (1831)

EDWARD VOGELGASANG, cabinetmaker, Howard Street south of Lombard (1840)

HERMAN VOLTGER, cabinetmaker, Light Street 1 door north of Hill (1840)

HARMAN WAGNER, cabinetmaker, Harford Avenue (1833)

JAMES WAINRIGHT, cabinet and chairmaker, 12 South Street (1807, 1808)

J. & T. WAINRIGHT, cabinetmakers, 67 South Street (1804)

JAMES P. WAKELEY, cabinetmaker, Pratt Street west of Caroline (1837); Light Street 1 door north of Hill (1840)

WALKER & GREWE, piano forte manufacturers, 3 East Street (1812)

I. F. WALKER, japanner, 19 McClettan's Alley (1840)

JOSEPH WALKER, cabinetmaker, Paca Street, west side north of Franklin (1824)

THOMAS B. WALKER, piano forte maker, 3 East Street (1814-15, 1816, 1817-18)

SIMON WALLER, cabinetmaker, 85 Bond Street south of Aliceanna (1840)

JAMES WALMSLEY, cabinetmaker, Market Alley south of Lexington Street (1835); 16 Eutaw Street, dwelling, Fayette Street east of Pine (1837); Saratoga Street 5 doors east of Green (1840)

HARMAN WALTER, cabinetmaker, Eutaw Street south of Camden (1835)

F. & H. WALTJEN, cabinetmaker, Sharp Street opposite Episcopal Church (1840)

JAMES WARD, cabinetmaker, 19 Comet Street, o.t. (1814-15); Caroline Street near Dulany (1816, 1817-18)

SAMUEL WARD, cabinetmaker, Barre Street 1 door east of Sharp (1840)

GEORGE WARFIELD, cabinetmaker, Sharp Street south of Lexington (1829); 33 S. Liberty Street (1831); 32 S. Howard Street (1833)

ANDREW WARKS, cabinetmaker, 37 Bridge Street, o.t. (1812)

WILLIAM WARNER, cabinetmaker, Henrietta Street near Charles (1837, 1840)

u

WILLIAM WATCH, chairmaker, Lee Street near Light, foot of f.h. (1829)

*WATSON & ETSCHBERGER, fancy furniture manufacturers, 49 South Street (1812)

THOMAS WATSON, turner and chairmaker, shop, 29 N. Gay Street, dwelling, back of 1 Baltimore Street (1810) ; dwelling, 38 N. Frederick Street (1812)

ARCHIBALD WATTS, chairmaker, S. Frederick Street (1800-01)

GEORGE WEAVER, cabinetmaker, 107 N. Eutaw Street (1831)

HENRY WEAVER, cabinetmaker, 15 Albemarle Street (1835) Gay Street adjoining Christ Church (1840)

JOHN H. WEAVER, cabinetmaker, 104 N. Eutaw Street (1833)

JOSEPH WEAVER, chair manufacturer, Paca Street south of Franklin (1829)

THOMAS WEBB, cabinetmaker, 8 Harrison Street (1829)

THOMAS WEDDERSTRAND, cabinetmaker, S. Frederick Street (1800-01, 1802) ; N. Calvert Street (1804, 1807, 1810)

JOHN I. WEISE, cabinetmaker, 5 N. Liberty Street (1824)

REUBEN WELLER, cabinetmaker, Saratoga Street east of Howard (1840)

THOMAS W. WELLS, cabinetmaker, 103 N. Howard Street (1822-23) ; Mulberry Street, north side east of Eutaw (1824)

NICHOLAS WEST, cabinetmaker, Forrest Street near the hay scales, o.t. (1819) ; North Street near East (1822-23, 1824)

SAMUEL WEST, cabinetmaker, 53 N. Gay Street (1810) ; 31 S. Gay Street (1812)

THOMAS WEST, cabinetmaker, W. Wilk Street near Granby, o.t. (1816)

THOMAS WHALEN, cabinetmaker, Washington Street south of Wilk (1837)

MR. WHEELER, cabinetmaker, 4 Cheapside (1835)

*ALLAN WHITE, ornamental painter, High Street, o.t. (1817-18)

PETER L. WHITE, cabinetmaker, 62 Pratt Street (1810, 1812, 1814-15, 1816) ; 12 W. Pratt Street (1819) ; 53 S. Calvert Street (1822-23)

WILLIAM WHITE, cabinetmaker, Baltimore Street west of Paca (1833)

CHARLES WHITELOCK, cabinetmaker, Baltimore Street east of Spring (1837)

*JOSEPH P. WHITING, ornamental painter, Front Street, east side south of Great York, o.t., dwelling, Comet Street, south side west end, o.t. (1824)

WILLIAM WIDDERFIELD/WINTERFIELD, cabinetmaker, Britton Street (1804) ; McElderry Street, o.t. (1812, 1814-15, 1817-18, 1819, 1822-23, 1824) ; Forrest Street north of Douglass (1827, 1829) ; 2 Forrest Street (1831, 1833, 1835)

HENRY WIEGEL, cabinetmaker, 4 Charles Street (1837) ; 4 Cheapside (1840)

FRANCIS WILLIAMS, cabinetmaker, 40 Harrison Street (1822-23)

JACOB WILLIAMS, chairmaker, shop, Public Alley (1800-01) ; back of 89 French Street, shop, Public Alley (1802, 1803, 1804) ; Pratt Street near the Falls (1807, 1808, 1810, 1814-15, 1816, 1817-18, 1819, 1822-23, 1824, 1827)

JAMES WILLIAMS, cabinetmaker, dwelling, Courtland Street near Saratoga (1833) ; 129 Hanover Street (1837, 1840)

JOHN WILLIAMS, cabinetmaker, 68 South Street, dwelling, 53 South Street, (1814-15, 1816) ; 66 South Street (1817-18) ; 66 & 68 South Street (1819) ; dwelling, Camden Street (1833)

v

JOHN and JAMES WILLIAMS, cabinetmakers, 68 South Street (1822-23)

THOMAS WILLIAMS, cabinetmaker, 52 N. Front Street (1831)

WILLIAM and MARICE WILLIAMS, chairmakers, 10 Pratt Street west of Bridge (1840)

WILLIAM WILLIAMS, chairmaker, 10 E. Pratt Street (1829, 1831, 1833, 1837)

JOHN WILSON, cabinetmaker, 47 Market Street, f.p. (1824)

JOSEPH WILSON, cabinetmaker, 60 Harrison Street (1807, 1808) ; Fountain Street, f.p. (1810) ; 52 Aliceanna Street, f.p. (1814-15) ; 15 Albemarle Street (1816, 1817-18) ; 46 N. Gay Street (1819) ; 48 N. Gay Street (1822-23)

THOMAS WILSON, cabinetmaker, 3 Tripolet's Alley (1800-01) ; joiner and cabinetmaker, back of 61 Baltimore Street (1802)

FRANCIS WINTER, cabinetmaker, corner of Mercer and Grant Streets (1840)

JOHN WISE, cabinetmaker, North Street south of Wagon Alley (1824)

KELLEY WISE, cabinetmaker, 9 Grant Street (1827, 1829)

FREDERICK WISOTSKY, piano forte maker, 33 S. Liberty Street (1808)

JACOB WITT, cabinetmaker, 66 South Street (1804)

GEORGE WITTBERGER, cabinetmaker, Guilford Alley, corner of Goodman Street, f.h. (1817-18)

PETER E. WOLF, cabinetmaker, 39 Water Street east of Gay (1827) ; Frederick Street South of Gay (1829)

*RICHARD WOLSEY, ornamental painter, 4 North Street (1833)

JOHN F. WOOD, chair factory, Hanover Street north of Pratt (1837) ; corner of Howard Street and Carpenter Alley, dwelling, Charles Street south of York (1840)

*FREDERICK WORKING, ornamental painter, Busy Alley near Charles Street (1831) ; E. Saratoga Street Street (1833)

CHARLES YAGER, cabinetmaker, 39 W. Wilk Street, f.p. (1812) ; W. Fleet Street, f.p. (1810)

E. and WILLIAM YEARLY, cabinetmakers, Bond Street, east side south of Bank, f.p. (1824)

EDWARD YEARLY, cabinetmaker, corner of Bond and Bank Streets (1827, 1829, 1831) ; 19 Gough Street (1833)

WILLIAM H. YEARLY, cabinetmaker, Caroline Street south of Bank (1835, 1837) ; 19 Gough Street (1840)

*FRANCIS YOUNKER, fancy chairmaker, 12 Baltimore Street (1807, 1808, 1810) ; 4 Baltimore Street, dwelling, Pitt Street (1812, 1814-15, 1816, 1817-18, 1819, 1822-23, 1824) ; 32 Water Street east of Comerce, dwelling, southwest corner of East and Pitt Streets (1827, 1829, 1833)

FREDERICK ZUGG, cabinetmaker, North Street, o.t. (1812)

W

SELECTED BIBLIOGRAPHY

Ackerman, Robert, ed. *The Repository of Arts, Literature, Commerce, Manufacture, Fashions and Politics.* London: 1809 to 1828.

Baltimore: The Baltimore Museum of Art, 1947. *Baltimore Furniture, The Work of Baltimore and Annapolis Cabinetmakers from 1760 to 1810.*

Baltimore. Maryland Historical Society. Dr. James Bordley, 1940.

Berkeley, Henry J. "A Register of the Cabinet Makers and Allied Trades in Maryland, as Shown by the Newspapers and Directories, 1746-1820." *The Maryland Historical Magazine,* XXV (March 1930) : 1-27.

Beunat, Josephe. *Recueil des dessins d'ornements d'architecture....* Paris: Sarrebourg & Paris, 1813.

Bjerkoe, Ethel Hall. *The Cabinetmakers of America.* Garden City, New York: Doubleday & Company, 1957.

Butler, Joseph T. *American Antiques 1800-1900: A Collector's History and Guide.* New York: The Odyssey Press, 1965.

The Cabinet-Maker and Upholsterer's Guide [Hepplewhite's Guide] ... from Drawings by A. Hepplewhite and Co., Cabinet-Makers. London: I. and J. Taylor, 1788; 2d ed., 1789; 3d ed., 1794.

Comstock, Helen, ed. *The Concise Encyclopedia of American Antiques.* 2 cols. New York: Hawthorn Books, 1958.

Comstock, Helen. *American Furniture, Seventeenth, Eighteenth, and Nineteenth Century Styles.* New York: The Viking Press, 1962.

Davidson, Marshall B. *The American Heritage History of American Antiques from the Revolution to the Civil War.* New York: American Heritage Publishing Co., 1968.

Groce, George C., and David H. Wallace. *The New York Historical Society's Dictionary of Artists in America, 1564-1860.* New Haven: Yale University Press, 1957.

Hall, John. *The Cabinet Maker's Assistant....* Baltimore: John Murphy, 1840.

Hope, Thomas. *Household Furniture and Interior Decoration, Executed from Designs by Thomas Hope.* London: Longman, Hurst, Rees and Orme, 1807.

Hutton, Amy. "Buchanan Family Reminiscences." *The Maryland Historical Magazine,* XXXV (September 1940) : 262-269.

Kimball, Marie G. "The Original Furnishings of the White House." *Antiques,* XV (June 1929) : 481-486.

Lawrence, A. W. *Greek Architecture.* Baltimore: Penguin Books, 1957.

Lockwood, Luke Vincent. *Colonial Furniture In America.* 2 vols. 3d ed. New York: Charles Scribner's Sons, 1926.

Meyer, Franz Sales. *Handbook of Ornament.* 4th ed. New York: Bruno Hessling, 1892.

Miller, Edgar G., Jr. *American Antique Furniture.* 2 vols. Baltimore: The Lord Baltimore Press, 1937.

Montgomery, Charles F. *American Furniture, The Federal Period,* in the Henry Francis du Pont Winterthur Museum. New York: The Viking Press, 1966.

Newark, New Jersey: The Newark Museum Association, 1963. *Classical America 1815-1845.*

New York: The Metropolitan Museum of Art, 1970. *19th-Century America, Furniture and Other Decorative Arts.*

Otto, Celia Jackson. *American Furniture of the Nineteenth Century.* New York: The Viking Press, 1965.

Percier, Charles, and Pierre F. L. Fontaine. *Recueil de Décorations Intérieures.* . . . Paris: Gidot L'aine, 1812.

Raley, Robert L. "Interior Designs by Benjamin Henry Latrobe for the President's House." *Antiques,* LXXV (June 1959) : 568-571.

Scharf, Col. J. Thomas. *The Chronicles of Baltimore.* Baltimore: Turnbull Brothers, 1874.

Semmes, John E. *John H. B. Latrobe And His Times 1803-1891.* Baltimore: The Norman Remington Co., 1917.

Sheraton, Thomas. *The Cabinet Dictionary.* London: W. Smith, King Street, 1803.

———. *The Cabinet-Maker and Upholsterer's Drawing Book.* London: Printed by T. Bensley, for W. Baynes, 1793; 3rd ed. revised, 1802.

———. *The Cabinet-Maker, Upholsterer and General Artists' Encyclopedia.* London: 1804-1806.

———. *Designs for Houshold Furniture.* London: J. Taylor, 1812.

Smith, George. *The Cabinet-Maker and Upholsterer's Guide: Being a Complete Drawing Book.* London: Jones and Co., 1826.

———. *A Collection of Designs for Household Furniture*

and Interior Decoration. London: J. Taylor, 1808.

———. *A Collection of Ornamental Designs after the Manner of the Antique.* London: J. Taylor, 1812.

Speltz, Alexander. *Styles of Ornament.* 2d ed. New York: E. Weyhe, 1910.

Varle, Charles. *A Complete View of Baltimore.* Baltimore: Samuel Young, 1833.

132

The details reproduced in the list of "Cabinetmakers and
Allied Tradesmens Working in Baltimore 1800-1840" are
from the following catalogue entries: a, cat. no. 25;
b, cat. no. 28; c, cat. no. 42; d, cat. no. 52; e & f,
cat. no. 55; g, cat. no. 41; h, cat. no. 28; i, cat. no. 36;
j, cat. no. 37; k, cat. no. 41; l, cat. no. 26; m, cat. no 29;
n, cat. no. 8; o, cat. no. 13; p, cat. no. 52; q, cat. no 6;
r, cat. no. 16; s, cat. no. 13; t, cat. no 20; u & v, cat. no 52;
w, cat. no. 59

Design: Omni Associates
Photography: Duane Suter
Composition: Service Composition Company, Inc.
Printing: Art Litho Company
Finishing: Graphic Arts Finishing Company